THE
SUCCESS
MAGNET

CULTIVATE THE 5 VALUES
THAT ATTRACT SUCCESS

ROY REDD

The Success Magnet™
Cultivate the 5 Values That Attract Success

Copyeditor
Wendell Anderson
NorthStar Writing & Editing

Visit the author's website at
www.royredd.com.

"Son, you're not like everyone else; you're different. I knew it since you were a little baby. You're going to do great things."

To my mother, who gave me the greatest gift anyone could give. The gift of belief in myself through consistent suggestion that I, one day, would be great.

THE

SUCCESS

MAGNET

CULTIVATE THE 5 VALUES THAT ATTRACT SUCCESS

TABLE OF CONTENTS

For if the willingness is there, the gift is acceptable according to what one has, not according to what he does not have.
—2 Corinthians 8:12 (New International Version)

ABOUT THE AUTHOR

Roy Redd is an author whose writings include Finish and The Success Magnet™: Cultivate the 5 Values That Attract Success. Roy helps people get out of their own way so they can be who they already are and achieve the results, and outcomes they desire.

Roy was blessed with certain struggles that made him realize he needed to take responsibility for his own life. Broke, depressed, and on his own, he ended up pushing his broken down car two miles on the freeway. That is when he realized nobody was to blame for his problems but himself. After that experience, and the gift of self-efficacy, Roy turned his life around. Roy went from broke to six figures in just a few short years.

Today, he works to motivate and teach others on how to turn their lives around. He is dedicated to sharing his story, successes, and how-tos so that others can achieve their goals. In addition, Roy coaches paying clients on how to get out of their own way so they can achieve their desired outcomes, successes, and dreams. He's been able to rub elbows with great people like Arnold Schwarzenegger, JT Foxx, Wayne Allyn Root, Joseph Michelli, and Donna Karan.

Roy's philosophy on life and business are unique. They are not based on the status quo, but on study and results. He is a true student of life and shares his perspective with inspiration and enthusiasm. Roy is truly dedicated to building a brand that helps others to succeed.

Get free value, and check out Roy at www.royredd.com.

@roy_redd   *@roy_redd*   *Roy Redd*

with Wayne Allyn Root
2008 presidential nominee

with Greg Reid author of
"6 Feet From Gold"

with Joseph Michelli author of
"The Starbucks Experience"

with Donna Karen

with Arnold Schwarzenegger

FOREWARD

"It takes courage to grow up to be who you really are."
—E.E. Cummings

I have the honor of preparing your mind to receive ideas that will shift your thinking for ultimate fulfillment and success in life through Roy's success attraction principles.

You see, we humans are a part of an ever-evolving society that shapes our thoughts and behaviors through its ideals and culture that may serve us sometimes but not at other times. We are at a time in our evolutionary history where discovering who we are meant to be and doing what we are designed for is challenging or nearly impossible. This is because we are unconscious to our abilities due to the societal programs that keep our minds limited and confined to work hard to bring about wealth and prosperity to a select few who run the social order. Because of this limited mindset, we often don't grow up into the people we imagined ourselves to be when we were young. We essentially become mentally fixed.

Roy discovered early who he wanted to be when he grows up. Like many of us, he wandered and got lost in the program of society. But he found his way out and is awakening other minds. I applaud this young man's fortitude to pull himself from the gravity of materialism, entertainment, and other distractions to see a bigger vision of himself filled with meaning. He, unlike many people, won't look back in life with regrets, challenges and all. He knows that each step in his journey serves as a piece of the puzzle to reaching his highest self.

In this book, he gives the keys to success. This book is his journey. It's his way of leaving footprints in the sands of society for those seeking to rise above the mental programs to improve their financial goals and overall potential. He is leading, in his own right, the next generation of mindsets to a place where even he may not know where the journey may lead. But at least, it is his own. He is the master of his fate.

I ask, as the student reading this book, to be open as he takes you on a mental odyssey of successful thinking and practice.

Shonté Jovan Taylor,
Neuroscientist, Entrepreneur, and Mindset Success Trainer

INTRODUCTION

SUCCESS AND HOW TO ACHIEVE IT

Success (n.): the achievement of a future ideal.

A beautiful flower is the flower that uses its gifts so that it can achieve its desired outcome. The vibrance and the sweetness of the flower's nectar are not for its own pleasure; they are so that the flower can attract the things it needs to bloom, such as butterflies and bees. Without the butterflies and the bees, the flower cannot be fruitful. Without the butterflies and bees, the flower cannot achieve its outcome and result. So, the flower, to attract what it needs, just becomes a better flower without movement. A flower attracts what it needs to be successful. A beautiful flower is a Success Magnet.™

Success is not a set of standards from our culture, but rather a collection of personal values clearly defined and ultimately achieved.

Most people think that success comes from luck, superhard work, or having some amazing talent. Yes, all of these things help in the attainment of success, but they are not the defining factors. Many people actually believe that they are having hardships because of outside forces bearing down on them. They believe that health, wealth, and happiness are preserved only for the rich. These things could 'not be further from the truth. In this book, I go to war with the idea of success coming from luck. I go to war with the traditional paradigms on how success is perceived and attained. I go on a relentless attack on the idea that success is something you chase.

The world is being pumped full of lies on how to achieve success and what brings happiness. Our recent ancestors taught us that going to school, getting a good job, and working 30 years or more until you retire is the path to all success and happiness. There is nothing wrong with that in any way. I know our parents and grandparents, worked their butts off to give us the opportunities we have today. But the world is changing. In today's world, it's harder and harder to get a job. School is more expensive and doesn't promise work shortly after. People aren't going for their dreams because they are afraid to leave the security of their jobs. People are working at jobs they hate just to barely get by.

There's more to life than just working 9 to 5 every day then partying on the weekend just to release the stress you've accumulated during the week. I know how it is. I've been there.

Everything I share in this book is opinion. I could be completely wrong. I often am. The principles I share in this book are based on the results I've obtained in my life, and the results many people have obtained in theirs. My ideas on how to achieve success may not pertain to you, but I ask you to read this book with an open mind—and an open heart.

I woke up one day, and life was terrible. I had no money. I had no car for transportation. And I just had broken up with my girlfriend. I blamed everybody else for my problems instead of taking responsibility for my own actions. I had truly made a lot of mistakes, and they were all starting to catch up with me. In a matter of weeks, I had lost my job, my car, my girl-friend, and all my money. I was in a bad place because of what I had decided to focus on. And I let life make me complacent as a person. One day everything just crashed. I had the worst day of my life. I was in such a bad place I had no choice but to change.

Success is the achievement of a future ideal, but you can achieve that ideal only if you cultivate your values.

Sometimes God sends you blessings wrapped up in a hard situation. Well, He sent me the gift of self-efficacy wrapped up in the worst time of my life. When I finally realized I wasn't living right, I changed the direction of my life. I was able to find out my problem and immediately started to fix it. You can't fix a problem in your life until you realize you have the problem, and I'm so blessed for my struggles—they showed me my issues. Within the next month, I doubled my income. I was able to save money, catch up on my bills, and secure my peace of mind. Within the next year, I doubled my income again, was able to purchase a brand new car, and met a wonderful woman who truly loves me. These aren't things that I set out to achieve; these are things that came into my life because of the person I had become. I realized everything in my life was a reflection of who I was. So it hit me—if my outside world was a reflection of who I had become, all I had to do was become a better person.

This book will show you how I was able to turn my life around in a matter of months. I've come to realize that if one person can do something, anybody can do it. It's possible for anyone, no matter where they are in life, to change the direction they are moving in. You can't change your destination in an instant, but you can change your direction.

You attract success by becoming an attractive person.

What if I told you that you don't need to chase success, but that success will find you? That you can become, what I call, a Success Magnet™? In the pages that follow, I give you the five major values that all of us should cultivate. If you work on these values in your life, success will come to you in abundance.

Let's say a guy who is a little overweight, not in shape, and doesn't work out tries to pick up on a woman who is in great shape, works out every day, and is gorgeous. What do you think is the possibility that she will be interested in him? Pretty low, right? The reason is she cultivates her value of fitness and health. Why would she be interested in someone who doesn't cultivate the same values? Or doesn't even believe in those values? Success is the same way. Success is looking for an attractive person to fall for. If success is looking for an attractive person to follow, the question is how do you become attractive enough for success?

The 5 Values Needed to Achieve Success
1. Money
2. Wisdom
3. Health
4. Love
5. Spirituality

Let's test it out. Quickly—think about five goals you have for your life. I'm willing to bet that you thought of a financial goal, a personal goal, a physical goal, a relationship goal or family goal, and a spiritual goal. If your goals were material goals, good luck chasing things rather

> *How much faith do you have to have to declare something that you are not sure is possible as if it were possible? Do you have the faith to put a time limit on such a declaration?*

than substance. I believe if you are able to work on these five areas of your life, success will come to you. All of a sudden, people will say how lucky you are and will marvel at the great things you have achieved.

I'm going to talk about the fundamentals in each of these areas that kick-started my successes. I'm going to share with you ideas, examples, and strategies on how to become more attractive in all of these areas. I'm going to show you how to become a Success Magnet.™

– *The 6 Human Needs*

I am so positive that these five values produce success as a whole because cultivating these values naturally supplies all your basic human needs. We humans have needs that are so strong we always find a way to acquire them. Some of the needs are more important to us than others, but we all have all six nonetheless.

The 6 Human Needs
1. Faith
2. Wonder
3. Importance
4. Affection
5. Improvement
6. Compassion

It could be in a positive way or a negative way; regardless, we find these needs. The key is to achieve these needs with intention in a way that serves you as a whole person.

– *Faith*

A lot of people are taught the wrong meaning of faith. Faith is not a belief, but an absolute certainty. People believe in things they are not absolutely sure of. But faith is having absolute certainty in something. When you walk outside, you don't believe in the ground; you have total faith that when you put your feet down, the ground will hold solid. Plenty of people who believe in themselves never become successful. Cultivating your values allows you to turn belief into faith, which is the fuel for achieving success.

– *Wonder*

Just like a kid, we wonder about so many things and are interested in all sort of subjects. We wonder about the earth. We wonder about space. We wonder about everything. We have this great wonder in which we set out to learn about our universe. This wonder has driven us to learn so much about the world. President John F. Kennedy had a big wonder about space and the moon. With that wonder, he applied faith when he said in 1961 "that we would go to the moon within 10 years' time."

A human's purpose seems to be to acquire knowledge. This need for wonder drives us to search for knowledge. First, we wonder about it. Then we form beliefs about it.

Then we set out to prove it. When you have proof about a belief, it is no longer a belief—it is now something you know. You now know what you first had wondered about.

How much faith do you have to have to declare something that you are not sure is possible as if it were possible? Do you have the faith to put a time limit on such a declaration?

- *Importance*

This is a very strong need. We all want to feel important and want others to think that we are important. That's why you're reading this book on success—being successful makes you feel important.

This human need depends on your lens of the world. The lens through with you view society determines what makes you important. Some think money makes them important. Some think love makes them important. Some think crime makes them important. If you're reading this book, your lens of the world is probably if I can be successful, I will be important. And rightfully so. But some people have a distorted lens that makes them think crime makes them important. Stealing makes a thief feel important. But achieving your dreams is what will make you feel important.

- *Affection*

The next human need, and one of the most powerful, is the need for affection. We all crave—some more than others—this need for affection. We desperately want affection from friends, from family, from a spouse, even from animals. We find affection and connection by either accident or intention. We all have seen homeless people with a dog they love dearly. The dog is the last form of affection they have a lot of the times. Remember, we will get these needs, no matter what the circumstance are. By applying the ideas in this book, you will learn to fulfill your need for affection, along with your other needs.

– *Improvement*

This is my favorite human need. We all want and need to improve and to grow as much as we can. I don't care what level of success you have if you are not improving, you will nothing be unhappy. If you are not improving the things that matter, you will not feel the charge that life requires of us. This problem can come into play when you achieve your dreams. Many people hit their biggest goal and then stop trying to improve because they have reached their outcome. The key is when you achieve a goal, you must always set new goals. When you realize your ideal, you must make new ideals for yourself. The need for improvement is a drive that challenges you and keeps you energized and happy.

– *Compassion*

The last basic need we have is the need to help others, compassion. This need is misunderstood greatly because of the way people ask for help. We love to help others when we actually believe we are helping them. We sometimes don't give to the homeless because we are not sure if we are actually helping them. We don't give to charity because we aren't sure we are helping the actual cause. And we don't give in church because we don't believe our money is being used for the proper cause. We love to give when we actually help someone. When we help others, we feel a beautiful connection to those we helped.

An extraordinary life is a life in which we wonder about something, have faith to strive to learn it, become successful by proving it, hit our goals and make new goals, keep loved ones in our lives, and use our success to help others.

THE 10 SUCCESS MAGNET™ COMMANDMENTS

1. Thou shalt have no values before thy own.
2. Thou shalt not make unto thee any graven image or likeness of anything that is not of thy personal values.
3. Thou shalt not hold thy dreams in vain, for no dream shall manifest in vain.
4. Thou shalt not let a day go to waste, for every day holds tremendous value.
5. Honor thy positives and thy negatives, for they both manifest thy knowing.
6. Thou cannot kill thee.
7. Thou cannot steal from thee.
8. Thou cannot commit idolatry.
9. Thou cannot covet what thou did not conceive.
10. Thou must take full responsibility for all that befalls thee in thy life.

– *Thou shalt have no values before thy own.*

Our values are the deepest convictions we have about ourselves. What we believe, what we love, what we know are valuable to us. I argue in this book that there are five major values that attract success. These are values that transform your being so that you are a better person, which will bring success naturally. The key is to put your values above all values. Never put anything before your health, your love, your growth, or your faith. Most people put their jobs, tangible tasks, and other people before their own values. For you to become the person you wish to become, you must never put anything before your own growth. This may sound selfish, but it's actually selfish if you don't give the world the value of your dreams. Never allow any distractions to dictate your focus and keep you from your success. Never compromise on your own values. Self-development is more noble then self-sacrifice—don't ever forget that. Thou shalt have no values before thy own.

- *Thou shalt not make unto thee any graven image or likeness of anything that is not of thy personal values.*

Never put anybody before your values leads me to this: never put anything before your personal values as well. Often times, people get caught up in things that have zero value whatsoever, such as material things. It's OK to have material things, and it's OK to want nice things, but these things should become a by-product of value delivered instead of obtaining these things thinking they bring value. Make the distinction between having things because they are valuable and having things making you feel valuable. Later in the book we explain why material things don't make you happy, but that money does make you happy if used properly. Don't think of your life as a race chasing material goods; rather think of it as a chase for growth in self, and material goods will be there anyway. When I was dead broke, I learned to be happy without the money, and the money came. Most people think they will be happy only when they have reached their success. Success does not make you happy; you become successful by being happy. Happiness is a choice, just like everything achieved in life is a choice. Make a choice now to cultivate your values and step into the giant vision you have for yourself. Thou shalt not make unto thee any graven image or likeness of anything that is not of thy personal values.

- *Thou shalt not hold thy dreams in vain, for no dream shall manifest in vain.*

This commandment should be self-explanatory. You can never achieve your dreams if you doubt them in any way that will cause you to quit. If you don't believe in your desired outcome fully, you won't achieve it. Better yet, if you don't know your desired outcome, you won't achieve it. In our culture, for reasons we won't talk about, people think that it's not OK to know, with total certainty, that they can achieve their dreams before they happen. When you know something, you don't need beliefs about it—you just know! Look at all the ultrasuccessful people in the world. They all knew what they were going to do as if it were already done.

That is faith. Faith is not the belief in what is not as if it were, but faith actually is total certainty in what is not as if it were. Knowledge is power, right? Well, what's the root word of knowledge? This is because your true personal power is in what you know. And I'm telling you now: you can know in your dreams instead of believing in them. Thou shalt not hold thy dreams in vain, for no dream shall manifest in vain.

- *Thou shalt not let a day go to waste, for every day holds tremendous value.*

We give away the true secret to discipline and habits later in the book. Most people know the importance of their habits but find it very hard to discipline themselves. We will teach you how to do that later in this book. Also, we break down what drives us and how to take the steering wheel to this vehicle. (For more on how to ignite ambition, go to RoyRedd.com and get my free ebook, Finish: 7 secrets to achieve your goals.) You must work on your values every day, just as you brush your teeth every day. Your health, your wisdom, your love, your spirituality should be attended to daily. This is why the first commandment is so important: when you cultivate your values, your time becomes mighty scarce. Remember, every day, never miss a day. Even if it's a small amount, get it done. Thou shalt not let a day go to waste, for every day holds tremendous value.

> – *Honor thy positives and thy negatives, for they both manifest thy knowing.*

What really gives you power and dictates your life is what you know. We are inspired and illuminated with knowledge to serve a purpose. Your dreams are an idea that was given to you with a great desire to achieve them. You can achieve them if you know you can. I know you can without even knowing you because I know that you would have never had the desire without the potential to achieve it. My job is to make you conceive this fact with the words in this book.

All knowledge is one. All ideas and knowledge is one great entity in which we conceive by becoming aware of it. People generally think of knowledge as something you obtain, but it is not. Knowledge is just there, but we can manifest it only by making our own concepts about it. For example: Most people think that Mozart was a great musician, that Picasso was a great painter, and that Socrates was an amazing philosopher. That is not the actual truth about these great people. The truth is that they had knowledge, and they conceived this knowledge and expressed it differently. To say that same sentence differently: they all were connected to knowledge, but they used different modalities to share the knowledge with the people. Mozart was a genius who had knowledge; music was just the modality he used to express this knowledge. Picasso, also a genius, had knowledge but used painting to express this entity. Socrates had knowledge and chose to put it into words and ideas.

When you conceived your dreams, you were also connected to knowledge, and whatever you desired to achieve is the modality you chose to express it.

Knowledge, to be manifested into the physical realm, must be put into motion. That is action. Action is the motion it takes to manifest your dreams. Knowledge is singular; it comes from one source. I don't know what you believe in, but I'm going to insert that all knowledge comes from God. Knowledge coming from God is perfect balance and perfect equilibrium. I say you have to put knowledge into motion because things that are balanced cannot be manifested. Knowledge is power, but in the physical realm, knowledge is only potential power if applied and acted upon. All concepts, to be manifested, must be put into motion, and all motion has its positive and negative opposites. For example: When you are illuminated with knowledge, the concept you come up with will always have its positive aspect and its negative aspect. This is the only way it can be manifested in the physical realm. The positives will be your inspiration and your confidence in the concept. The negative aspect is your doubts and fears about the concept. The important part is to realize that both of these are for good because they both manifest what you know. They both manifest your knowing. Honor thy positives and thy negatives, for they both manifest thy knowing.

- *Thou cannot kill thee.*

Contrary to what the general consensus believes, you

cannot be killed. Nobody can kill your dreams. Nobody can kill your peace of mind. Nobody can kill your character. Only you can do that. Generally, people allow outside forces to kill them and cause them to have dream death, peace-of-mind death, and character death. You will always have negative aspects of all things, but nothing can kill them but you. Only you can kill yourself and give up. If your dream dies, it is no one's fault but yours. Most people have excuses for why they let their dreams die. Excuses are a solid foundation to stand on when you decide to quit, without admitting that you quit. People have the most excuses from the lack of money, the lack of time, or the lack of knowledge, but, of course, they are just excuses. When you make a decision, when you just decide to do something, there is nothing that can stop you—except you. Thou cannot kill thee.

- *Thou cannot steal from thee.*

If I told you that it is impossible for anyone to steal from you, you might tell me that things get stolen all the time. But the thing is, things aren't real, and they hold no true value. Nobody can steal the only thing that really matters, and that is what a person can conceive. Nobody can steal your concepts, your ideas, or your thoughts. The modality that you use to represent an idea can be mimicked but not stolen. Only you have the vision for whatever you decide to build. And only you can master it. We can't steal anything that doesn't correspond with the level of our consciousness.

For example: If somebody steals money from you, yes, they got that money, but things will quickly go back to how they were. You earned the money, and you can earn that amount of money again, but the person who stole the money will spend it and not have any money later due to a lack of knowledge of how to attain it. If he knew how to attain it in the first place, he would not have stolen it. Stealing is trying to obtain something in which we don't have the awareness to attain, which is impossible to do. I can't steal anyone's brain or the hard work they put in to acquire something. Whatever comes to you, whatever happens to you, whatever surrounds you will be in accordance with the person you are, no matter who or what tries to stop it. When you become better, and cultivate the law of being, you will be a success magnet and success will come. Nothing will stop it. Thou cannot steal from thee.

- *Thou cannot commit idolatry.*

You cannot idolize anything that is not within the ideal that you created for yourself. Don't idolize these superficial paradigms that society says is success, but idolize what success is for you. Your inner corresponds with the outer, and you cannot correspond your inner to someone else's outer. Physically, mentally, and spiritually we can conceive only our own ideals and reflect our own outer appearance. It's like an eagle being raised with ducks. He can't idolize a duck because the eagle was meant for a much different ideal. Just as an eagle can't be a duck, you can't take ducks to eagle school. Like attracts like, so when you conceive your ideal and become that person, you will naturally attract the people, the finances, and all the success that matches up. Thou cannot commit idolatry.

- *Thou cannot covet what thou did not conceive.*

You cannot yearn or desire for that which someone else conceives. If you do this, you are being jealous and are desiring to have what is impossible for you to obtain. Admiring is OK, and loving the beauty of someone else's concept is fine, but desiring to have it is jealousy. There is no point in even wanting someone else's concepts because it's impossible for you to conceive their ideals. Your ideal may be similar, but it won't be identically the same. There are 7 billion people on this earth, and we all have a different point of view from which we perceive the universe. Our viewpoint is our personal power, and this power is personal for a reason. There is no point in trying to have someone else's viewpoint because it is impossible anyway. Thou cannot covet what thou did not conceive.

- *Thou must take full responsibility for all that befalls thee in thy life.*

It is my ambition, my dream to inspire and instruct millions on how they can consciously co-create their own experiences with intention. I know that this is the next evolution for us as a species, and I will assist all that I can to achieve this. The thing is, you can't create your own experiences until you first take full responsibility for your life. How can you create something if you don't believe you are in full control? You can't. It takes courage to drop the excuses and take responsibility for your life. It takes courage to stand in front of a empty canvas and create from nothing. But until you take responsibility, you can never create what you want. The problem is, most people are driving the vehicle of life and not taking responsibility for their accidents. They blame all the other drivers on this road because they don't want to look in the mirror and tell themselves when they fail. They are running away from their own power, just because they don't want to admit when they screw up. It took the worst screw-up of my life for me to finally realize this. It took being broke, depressed, and embarrassed for me to realize this truth. But when I did, my life changed dramatically and quickly. I invite you to do the same. I invite you to take full responsibility for your life. I invite you to stand in front of a blank canvas and, with intention, create your ideal life. Thou must take full responsibility for all that befalls thee in thy life.

CHAPTER 1

THE WORLD

MONEY

Let's look at the current states of these topics. First, let's look at money. I always start with money not because it's most important, but because it's the easiest thing to measure. To become better at anything, you must first find out where you stand. With money, it's easy to figure out where you stand because all you have to do is count. In November 2012, the U.S. Census Bureau posted that more than 16 percent of the population lived in poverty in the United States, including almost 20 percent of American children, which is about 44 million people. California, where I live, has a poverty rate of 23.5 percent, the highest in the country.

Poverty, according to the Consumer Price Index, is based on total income received. The level for 2012 was set at $23,050 total income annually for a family of four. There are roughly 643,000 sheltered and unsheltered home-less people nationwide. Around 44 percent of homeless people are actually employed. In America, where there is more opportunity than any other country, why is this happening?

I believe there are several reasons. For one, people have no idea where money comes from and how it is accumulated. Secondly, people have no idea how or 'don't have the discipline to save money. Financial freedom is a goal that I believe everyone should seek. Studies have shown that money does affect happiness—until you have reached the average income of the country. Then it has little effect on happiness. The new approach that's need-ed is to become educated on how money is made, how to make more, and how to allocate it properly.

WISDOM

Wisdom (n.): the quality of having experience, knowledge, and good judgment.

Now let's look at wisdom. I understand wisdom comes from your own experience, but it also comes from other people's experiences. Albert Einstein said, "A smart person learns from his own mistakes, but a genius learns from other people's mistakes."

One way I was able to learn what I needed to know to turn my life around was by reading. One book can shave years off your learning curve. The average person reads three books in a lifetime. That's a ridiculous statistic, and it's quite sad. It seems as though the only time people read today is if they have to because of school or if they're reading a fictional book. It's rare for people to actually read books just to learn on their own.

Let me ask you a question: if you needed a tutor for, let's say, math, would you hire someone who has a degree in mathematics, or would you hire someone who reads books on math constantly and is committed to mastery of that subject? The most logical answer is the person who is committed to mastery, right? Someone who goes to school to get a degree in that area may study only during school and never study again. But someone who is committed to mastery is on a lifelong commitment to learning and stretching his skills.

There is very little difference between someone who can't read and someone who doesn't read, and the result of both is ignorance.

King Solomon is said to have been the wisest man to ever live. God told Solomon he could have one wish, any wish he wanted, and Solomon wished for infinite wisdom. Solomon 'was not only the wisest person to ever live but also the richest. So if Solomon didn't ask for riches, but asked instead for wisdom, and riches came with it, that just proves the importance of becoming a wise person.

HEALTH

Health might be the most important value to first cultivate. If you are not healthy, you will not be able to work on any other of your values. If you're too sick to get out of bed, there isn't any way you can have the vibrancy and enthusiasm it takes to discipline yourself to become a more valuable person.

Unfortunately, we live in a time where people are more sick, overweight, and lethargic than ever. According to the Centers for Disease Control, some 35.7 percent of U.S. adults are obese. Conditions that come from obesity include heart disease, stroke, type 2 diabetes, and all types of cancers. Almost 41 million woman and 37 million men over the age of 20 were obese, by an actual survey done in 2010. I've worked in the medical field for ten years, and I've seen the effect this has on people's lives. I worked on an ambulance for the first five years of my working life.

One day we were called out to a woman having breathing problems. When we get there, I smell feces and urine everywhere.

I walk up to introduce myself. "Hi, my name is Roy. What seems to be the problem today?"

In a very gaspy voice she says, "I can't breath."

I immediately put her on oxygen to help her breathing while I ask her some questions. As I'm questioning her, I think about how are we were going to get this lady out of this house. She 'hasn't moved from her bed in a year—and she weighs 650 pounds! This woman literally ate herself to this point, in her bed, during the last year. To make things 10 times worse, we are on the sixth floor of an apartment building!

As we pull her down the stairs and put her in the ambulance, I say, "Ma'am, you deserve to live better than this. I know I'm young, and I don't mean to be disrespectful, but you deserve to live vibrant so that you can be present for your kids as they grow older."

She starts to cry. "Yes, I know," she replies.

I grasp her hand and pray with her as I've done with a lot of my patients.

Four months later I was at the mall when that same lady walked up to me and gave me the biggest hug. I didn't even recognize her. She had lost 200 pounds, and, although she was still big, it was OK because she was now able to walk. She thanked me and said that nobody had ever told her what she needed to hear. I don't know how that lady is doing now, but I'm sure she kept losing weight and is living much better than she was before.

I know you may not be overweight or obese, but to feel

vibrant and to have the energy needed to succeed, you must pay close attention to your health and fitness.

LOVE

Love is self-explanatory. Love is the most powerful force known to humans. It is no coincidence that love is at the forefront of all religions and spiritualities. Love has changed lives and has defeated hate at its highest levels. Love is vital to your mind, body, and soul. The more love you have, the healthier you are physically, and emotionally. The less love you have, the more likely you are to be depressed and have problems with stress.

Feeling unloved is one of the major causes of depression. A paradigm in our culture says that love just happens, and so depressed people sit around waiting for love to find them. Any value you wish to cultivate is first a study. Then it is a practice. Yes, even love. Love is first a study on what is love. Then it is a practice on how to love.

For entertainment, pop culture displays unrealistic images of how love happens. The problem is people start to believe in these unrealistic portrayals of how love happens. Then, when we find love, we are shocked to find out what it really is because it doesn't fit the ideal we first had about it. We want that super-romantic love that television, movies, and songs portray. But that isn't true love. It is necessary to change your thoughts on what love is so that you are not disappointed.

Today, more people are searching for love in the wrong

areas. Divorce rates are higher than ever because people expect love to be easy. There are always differences between people; that's just how the world is. 'No one out there 'is exactly like you and just perfect for you.

When I explain true unconditional love, I talk about kids. Parents love

Love is not a feeling. Love is an action. It is something you work on and show by how you act.

their children, no matter what. Their kids don't have to be the cutest, the smartest, or the best at anything, but they still love them unconditionally. You love your kids with all of their faults. That's what true love is.

SPIRITUALITY

Religion (n.): an institutionalized system grounded in belief and worship.

Spirituality (n.): a sensitivity or attachment to religious values.

Believing in a higher power is essential for organization in human life. People need to believe in a higher ideal that a supreme being governs this universe. Whatever you believe in, I believe you must study it, practice it, and preach it. The importance of spirituality is vital to all success. Being in tune with who you are and what you believe—and living in congruence with those beliefs—is important to living a successful life.

I want to point out that spirituality and religion are two different things. Religion is communal and implies adherence to an external structure of morality and belief system. In other words, religion is an outside structure that you follow based on your beliefs.

Spirituality is a different concept. Spirituality is more about what you believe in and what are your values. All values must be protected, especially spiritual values. I'm not saying that any specific beliefs are better than any others. I'm simply saying that whatever your beliefs are, make sure you cultivate them. Spirituality is personal. Spirituality is the freedom of belief. It implies believing in something and living by a set of principles.

You must say and do the things you actually believe because the things you say and do are symbols of who you are.

A lot of people have a set of principles they believe in, but they don't live in congruence with these principles. The law of congruence says that whatever we believe in, we must live in line with those beliefs or we will never be happy.

If you believe in helping others, but you never help others, this is a bad use of the law of congruence. That's why I share strategies in this book on how to cultivate your own spirituality as best as you can.

WINNER AND LOSERS

The winners and the people who are going to succeed

in today's world are the people who stop chasing success. As Jim Rohn said, "Don't chase success. What you chase eludes you." Instead, become a successful person. If you focus on the person you have to become, instead of chasing the things you want, everything you want will come to you. This is what being a Success Magnet™ is all about—cultivating the five major values that attract the success you want. You can be, do, or have anything you wish if you accept this philosophy. If you cultivate the five values of money, wisdom, health, love, and spirituality, nothing will stop your dreams from coming true.

– *Winners*

The people who become Success Magnets™ are the people who ...

> ❖ ***Respect money.*** They are the people who save and allocate their money properly. They are the people who learn to bring more value to the marketplace because they understand how money is accumulated.

> ❖ ***Commit to constant learning.*** They are the people who realize they are one idea away from doubling their income. They are the people who know that ideas come from information, so they read daily. They are the people who go to classes and attend seminars.

❖ *Work out and eat healthy to protect their body from disease.* They are the people who are enthusiastic, and their body has the energy to take on life.

❖ *Don't practice hate; they spread love.* They spread love to their companions, their family, to the world.

❖ *Live in congruence with their highest ideals* and spread their beliefs far and wide.

Success is looking for a beautiful home to live in, and that home is a place built from a foundation of strong values.

- Losers

The losers in today's world are the people who believe success is something you chase. They never come from a place of being, and they wonder why they can't reach their goals. One of the worst feelings in life is having above-average goals but being a below-average person. If you set a goal to be physically fit, for example, you must first ask yourself is, who do I have to be to achieve this goal? Most people say, "OK, to be fit, I have to go to the gym, and I have to eat better." This is true, but there's no vision in this way of thinking. If you come from a place of being, and ask yourself who you have to be to achieve this goal, knowing how comes much easier.

To achieve any goal, you need two essential things to drive you toward its attainment: motivation and education. If you have only one of the two, chances are you won't succeed. You can know how to do something intellectually, but if you aren't motivated to do it, you won't achieve it. For example: smokers know that smoking is bad for them, yet they still smoke. Why is that? It's because they have no motivation to stop smoking. If they go to the doctor and the doctor gives them a month to live if they continue to smoke, chances are they will quit. The difference is now they have the motivation to quit that goes with what they already knew.

Let's talk about being motivated without being educated. A person can have all the motivation in the world but have no clue what she is doing. I can scream and shout about making more money, but if I don't know how, there is no way I can do it. Jim Rohn famously said, "You can't just be motivated, but you have to be educated. If you are motivated and not educated, then you are just a motivated idiot." You need both education and motivation.

MY SOLUTION SEARCH

After the day that changed my life, I decided to fix things, no matter what it took. I read book after book after book on success. I went to seminars and listened to motivational audio programs trying to learn how to be a more successful person.

One day I was at work on my break reading a self-help book when a friend of mine asked me what was I reading. I showed him the book, and it sparked a conversation between us, sharing our goals and ambitions. He told me he had a life coach and that his coach was throwing a seminar in Los Angeles the next month. I had no money to pay for the ticket, so I kind of brushed it off. The next day we spoke again, and he told me he had an extra ticket and invited me to go.

At the seminar, I'm very nervous. I have never been around so many successful people before. "Roy, just smile and speak up," I tell myself. "Be confident."

I'm standing at the front door when an older man comes up to me and says, "You look happy. What's your name?"

""I tell him.

"Is this your first time here, Roy?"

"Yes," I reply, with a big smile.

He welcomes me with open arms and invites me to eat dinner with him later.

The seminar is amazing. I learn more in the first hour about success than I had learned in my whole life. I meet and exchange contact information with authors, speakers, and the world's best success coaches. I'm so excited to meet them. What's so cool is they are excited to meet me as well!

Later at dinner, the older fellow I had met earlier tells me what he did and shares some of his success secrets. I listen, but I'm not ' fully present because I figure this guy just loves to talk. "And that's why I'm worth 1.6 billion dollars today," he says.

My eyes open wide. "What? Wait, did you say 1.6 billion dollars?" I ask.

With a straight face he calmly says, "Yeah, well it was 2.5, but we took a hit when the economy went bad."

From this point on, my ears are wide open. I instantly become interested in all he has to say. And, boy, does he have a lot to say. He tells me how to get the most out of the seminar and to make sure I took great notes.

That's exactly what I had done, and it has helped my life tremendously. In that one seminar, I met probably a dozen millionaires and three billionaires. What caught my attention was what they all had to say about success began to sound redundant. They all had the same philosophies on how to attain success. I started to see a trend. What finally hit me was they all worked on certain things to become successful and had certain ways of thinking. So, I told myself to learn as much about these things as I could and, maybe, I could be successful as well.

And that's exactly what I did.

CHAPTER 2

LIFE'S LESSONS

HOME AND SCHOOL

I had the best childhood ever. I was spoiled. I got what I wanted, when I wanted it, how I wanted it. My mother and father made life really easy for me. They did very well for themselves and made sure I had the opportunities they didn't. I was the biggest mama's boy and still am in many ways. My mom got me the latest video games, the latest clothes, and all the latest toys. She's pretty much done this my whole life. My mom and dad separated when I was nine years old. Even though they were not together, my parents did an amazing job of working together to keep me educated, disciplined, and taken care of growing up.

As a kid, I was never great in school, not because I wasn't smart, but because I didn't like school. The only reason I got by was because I needed a certain grade point average to play basketball. If it wasn't for my love for basketball, I can't say for sure I would have graduated high school.

The fact that I didn't have great grades eventually made me feel like I wasn't smart. Our culture is set up on people basing your intelligence on how good your grades are, which is the wrong measurement.

When I was 12, my mom remarried, and we moved about a hour away from my dad. The new school I went to was much harder because the kids were different, and the academics were much tougher. The basketball team wasn't great, so, naturally, I hated being there. My mother then decided that in my junior year of high school that I could move back with my father, so that's what I did.

I was back at a school that was easier and had a good basketball team. While living with my father, I learned from watching him what hard work and dedication really was. Every day he woke up at 4 a.m. to the sound of country music and went to work. He worked from 5 a.m. to 11 p.m., came home, and read till at least 1 a.m. Then he took a three-hour nap, got up, and went to work again. I saw my dad do this for the two years I lived with him.

Because school was easier and I was playing basketball, my grades improved, not because I was smarter or worked harder, but just because it was easier.

The last two months of my senior year I moved back with my mother. Certain high schools require more credits to graduate than other schools do. Because I had moved back with my mom, the school I was in required more credits than the school I had come from. This made me a whole semester short in credits to graduate high school. I was forced to take occupational classes at night just to graduate on time. The only class available was a class for emergency medical technician. This class was by far the hardest class the whole district had to offer. Thirty people started the class. Twelve people graduated, and six of those twelve were repeat students.

Although this class was extremely difficult, I made it through. I loved the idea of helping people, so I had no problem studying and learning the material—I wanted to learn. At the end of the class, I not only passed and received the credits I needed, but I also received a certificate to practice as an EMT in the state of California. I walked away with a lot of life lessons from that class. I learned how to work well under pressure and how you can't be complacent when it comes to saving someone's life. At 17 years old, I had graduated from high school and became an emergency medical technician in the state of California.

I applied for a job at an ambulance company as soon as I finished school, and they hired me on the spot. I learned a lot of skills, made what I thought was a lot of money at the time, and moved out of my mother's house into an apartment. The money I was making made it easy to pay my bills, so I never really budgeted at all. I would buy all the new Nikes that came out, latest fashions, nice watches, and all those material things just because I had extra money. Also, I knew that if I needed a little extra money, my mother would bail me out. I had no clue how to save. And even if I had, I didn't have the discipline to save anything. I started to become comfortable. I wasn't progressing toward anything, and I had nothing to show for my work. I figured I was doing well because I was making more money than all of my peers were, so I saw no need to progress toward anything.

Human beings are purposeful. We are happy only when we are moving forward toward a certain goal, and I wasn't doing that. Either we are growing or we are dying. There's no such thing as sitting still. I was dying. I got into this rhythm of going to work, on the weekends going to the club and partying, and then starting all over. I wasn't working on my values or chasing any sort of goal at all.

MY STRUGGLE

Then a chain of events happened. In the next couple of months, I lost my job, my car broke down, and I broke up with my girlfriend at the time. Life has a funny way of making you progress if you're sitting still.

I drove into work one day and my boss was outside waiting for me. In his hand, he had my last check. "Redd, here is your last check," he said. "You have five minutes to grab your things and leave."

I was extremely upset because I really enjoyed my job, and, quite frankly, I was the best at it in that whole company. Once you've worked as an EMT, it's generally easy to get a job, so I was able to get a new job within a week. It didn't pay as much as my previous job, but it was a job.

Within the next week, my truck broke down, so I 'had no transportation. My brother ended up letting me have his car, which looked like a hearse. It was an all-black 1990 station wagon that he no longer was driving.

The next two years I bounced from job to job barely having enough money to pay my bills. Then I landed a job that I liked again. It was at an ambulance company owned by firemen. They were all about helping their employees. They gave me the schedule I wanted and really took me in as a member of the fraternity. I worked there for a few months until bad luck hit me again. Something went wrong with the company, and they had to close down for a while until they could get back up and running. They told us employees what had happened and said they would be glad to hire us back in a few months when they took care of business.

I couldn't wait on them. I needed a job to keep up with my bills. I landed a job at this terrible ambulance company. This company was the worst ambulance company I had ever seen. 'The company had substandard equipment, treated employees poorly, and paid a pitiful salary. I was behind on bills and had no money, so I took the job temporarily.

Driving home one day, my car broke down again. I had just got this new crappy job an hour away from where I lived and had no way to get there. I towed the car home, called the junk man, and sold it $300. I added that $300 to the only money I had, which totaled $500, and bought a beater car.

To make things worse, the girl I was with at the time, I found out, was sleeping with multiple men to get back at me. My mother was upset with me and not talking to me, so I had nobody to ask for help. Life was terrible. I had never imagined that all these things could go bad at once.

THE DAY THAT CHANGED MY LIFE

The way I was living attracted these things to come into my life. I was driving a bucket of a car, working at a job I hated, and was stressed out and depressed for months. I stopped hanging out with friends because I had no money, plus I didn't want them to see how I was living. Then one day everything changed.

It's a cold winter morning. I'm having a nightmare about working at a terrible job, driving a bucket for a car, and having no money in the bank.

Then I hear this voice speak to me. "Roy," it says. "Get up."

I'll never forget that voice. It was almost as though it were saying, "Get up. Today your life is going to be changed."

I wake up and realize my nightmare is a reality. I get up lethargically, walk into the bathroom, quickly brush my teeth, throw on my uniform, and head to work. It's 35 degrees outside, and I have no heater in my 1987 Honda

Civic that barely runs. I hate this car. It's an ugly beige color and smells like cigarettes. Most of my friends don't know that I drive this piece of junk. I refuse to go anywhere but to work and back in this thing.

I scrape the ice off of the windshield, jump in, and drive off. I live in the Inland Empire but work in Los Angeles, about an hour away, two hours in traffic. I drive as fast as I can because I'm running late. I have no music in my car, so I have to listen to my thoughts the whole way. I'm actually making good time until I hit traffic on the 10 Freeway heading west. There's no way I'm going to make it to work on time in this traffic. Frustrated, and with my boss's nagging voice in my head—"If you're late again, I'm going to write you up"—I decide to jump into the diamond lane. I'm afraid to drive in the diamond lane by myself in this car because it has no tinted windows. The ticket for driving in the diamond lane in California is $297, if you're caught.

I'm a thinker, so I figure if I take the diamond lane every day and get caught only twice a year, it will be well worth the money.

Anyway, I'm driving along, the diamond lane is moving fast, and I'm making great time. I'm going to make it. Then all of a sudden, I smell smoke. I look down at my engine. (In this car, nothing separates the engine from the front seat.) I see small flames and smoke. The car dies. I jump out of the car.

"This can't be happening," I say to myself.

I'm stuck on the 10 Freeway in the diamond lane at 6:30

in the morning in 35-degree weather with hundreds of cars behind me honking their horns. At first, I look for someone to help me as I have done my whole life. I look at the lady behind me for help, but she 'doesn't want to push my car in her new Mercedes and scratch her bumper. She just looks at me and shruged her shoulders. On the 10 Freeway, the diamond lane is separate from the freeway. There 'isn't any turn-off lane, so I'm stuck. Embarrassed and scared to get a ticket, I decide to push the car until there is a turn-off point. I hear a helicopter above me. It's the Channel 7 news chopper showing me on TV because I'm the person holding up traffic. I am embarrassed. I see a turn-off point about two and a half miles down. Full of adrenaline that came from the embarrassment, I push and push and push. I get some momentum and just keep my head down in fear of the world looking at me. I'm mad at everyone and everything.

"People are so selfish," I say to myself. "This lady won't even help me push with her car."

Then it hits me. I realize I am in this position because of my bad choices. 'Nobody's fault but mine that I am in this predicament. When I realize this, I start to cry. "This will never happen again. No matter what, I'm going to get my life together," I say in a powerful voice.

SINCE THAT DAY

After that day, I was a completely different person. That experience made me realize that I needed to take full responsibility for what happens to me. When you decide to take full responsibility for your life, you truly step into adulthood. With this new philosophy on life, I decided to live better and learn everything I needed to know to fix my situation. And that's exactly what I did.

That first month I got a better job that not only paid more but also was a job I loved. I doubled my income almost overnight. I went to the car dealer and bought a brand new car, with a heater and a working CD player. I caught up on all of my bills and actually had money to save. My life did a complete turn around in a matter of weeks. Since that day, I have doubled my income annually every year, have met the love of my life, and have lived more congruent with my values. Things just started going my way. It was almost as if I no longer needed to chase my goals—my goals were chasing me.

This all took place in 2010. Since then, my life has dramatically improved in all areas. I was able to increase my income in a matter of a few short months. I learned how money was made and how to bring value to people to make more. I also learned how to manage my money so that I can save for the present and the future.

In 2011, I was in a learning phase. I was able to pick up some great ideas and become a lot wiser. I met new great friends who were on the same journey as I was trying to become great people. Life did a complete 180. I was now moving toward the purpose for my life. In 2012, things kept going well. I was able to double my income again by becoming full time at my job and getting paid more. I started to learn new great philosophies of life and happiness. I was

Life is about improvement and progression. If you're not getting better as a person, you won't feel fulfilled, and you won't attract what you want.

able to weed out all the last bits of negativity and bad things holding me back from going further.

In 2013, things got even better. I doubled my income once more by taking action on some ideas I had. I have a solid business partner who makes sure I stay accountable and moving toward my goals. I wrote down my goals for 2013 at the end of 2012.

As I write this book, I'm happy to say I have achieved all of my goals financially, physically, and emotionally for that year. The awesome thing about achieving your goals is it gives you the confidence to set big bold new goals that will stretch you and your skills. For being a 26-year-old kid, I have made and saved a good amount of money. I can honestly say that as far as my financial goals, I have achieved them all. I don't say that to brag; I say that to prove a point and because I'm proud of what I have done. I am blessed for the struggles I've had. The average income of Americans is $30,000 a year. I'm glad to say I tripled that this year. I'm not a millionaire or have crazy success yet, but I have achieved a level of success in a short amount of time by acting on the ideas I am going to share. I was able to go from broke to six figures in three short years.

But enough about me. Let's now get down to it and break down the things that can make "you" a Success Magnet™.

CHAPTER 3

HOW I DID IT

OBSTACLES

Before we get into the breakdown on how to cultivate each of these values, let's talk about obstacles. In anything you do in life, you will run into obstacles that can either make you quit or make you stronger. With competence comes confidence, so I'm going to show you the obstacles you're going to face beforehand. That way you can move forward with confidence because you have the competence to know what will get in your way. I want to talk about some obstacles that you might run into, and how you can defeat them.

Obstacles to Success
  1. Beliefs
  2. Poor planning
  3. Lack of resources

– Beliefs

Belief (n.): the mental act, condition, or habit of placing trust or confidence in something.

The No. 1 obstacle you must overcome before you can achieve anything is believing you can do it. If you don't believe you can do something, you won't act to do it. If you don't act, you will never reach your potential. If you never reach your potential, you will never attract the results you want in life. When you believe in yourself, and your abilities, nothing can stop you from achieving your goals.

Think about something you have achieved in your life that is significant to you. If you hadn't believed you could do that, would you have even tried?

When I think of belief, I think of a Bible story. I'm not an expert on the Bible, but I read it because it has great examples on life. In the story, the disciples were all in a boat when they saw Jesus walking toward them on the water. At first, they were nervous, thinking they saw a ghost because they did not believe anyone could walk on water.

> But Jesus immediately said to them: "Take courage! It is I. Don't be afraid." "Lord, if it's you," Peter replied, "tell me to come to you on the water." "Come," he said. (Matthew 14:27-29; New International Version)

Without a doubt in his mind that it was Jesus, Peter stepped onto the water and walked toward Jesus and met him in the middle of the lake.

When I think about this story, I take away one big lesson. Could Peter have ever walked on the water if he had not believed? Or, better yet, would he ever have taken a step onto the water at all if he didn't believe? The answer to both questions is no. If he never believed he could, he would never have stepped onto the water.

– *Action*

If you don't believe, you will never take action. Action is the work that you have to do to bring your dreams into life. Dreams can be facts if you act; it's all up to you. If your dreams were a destination, and you are the means of transportation, action is the fuel that gets you there.

So many people have big dreams, great ideas, and great inventions, but they never act. What's the point of being a great thinker or having an amazing idea if you're not going to plant the seed to bring it into fruition? Jim Rohn said, "Don't let your learning lead to knowledge. You'll become a fool. But let your learning lead to action and you can become wealthy."

In his book Crossing the Unknown Sea, David Whyte talked about how he was working at a job but had a vision to make money by writing poetry. He 'did nothing to make the first move toward this vision, so he started to feel unhappy. He told his friend about his unhappiness. His friend told him that you can't just visualize your dream; you have to act on it. He called it wholeheartedness. After that day, David started taking small steps toward his vision. They weren't major steps, but he was acting. Every day he worked on his poems and made phone calls trying to find places to speak. After 273 days, he got a call from a conference coordinator who had had a speaker cancel. He wanted David to come to read his poetry to fill the void. David read an amazing poem, which eventually led to his speaking to cooperate America and later earning a six-figure annual income. David knew what he wanted to do but never took the action required until he was inspired by a friend. Imagine if David never had taken any action steps. He would never be where he is today, and his vision would have died inside of him.

The best kind of action is inspired by motivation, the kind of motivation from your heart that ignites something that resonates with you. Action driven by motivation will bring you to any destination you wish to go.

– Potential

Potential (n.): the inherent ability or capacity for growth.

If you don't act, you will never reach your potential. I believe everyone should strive to achieve their potential. The crazy part about potential is that as human beings, our potential is unlimited. When it comes to growth, people have no bounds. You can stretch and become better at anything if you just work at it. We are like sponges: we can absorb anything we wish if we just put the work in to do it. It is impossible to use up all the memory in your brain. No one in history has ever even come close to being so smart that 'he wasn't able to learn more.

When I think of potential, I think of Michael Jordan. Growing up, Mike wasn't the best natural basketball player. He had to work and hone his skill and abilities to become better. When Mike was in high school, he was cut from his varsity basketball team. His coach told him he had the potential to be good, and he would let him play next year if he worked out with the team every morning. And that's exactly what M.J. did. He committed to becoming the best basketball player he could be from that point on. He ended up making the team that next year and going on to college on a full scholarship. He went on to play at North Carolina and then to the NBA. He is now known worldwide for being the best basketball player to ever play. He had no clue what his potential was or how good he could be, but he just knew he was going to be the best he could be.

– *Results*
Results (n.): an outcome from particular actions, operations, or courses.

If you are not reaching your potential, you will never achieve the results you want in life. When it comes to trying to achieve anything in life, results are the only thing that matters. When you set out to do something, you are trying to achieve a desired result. Achieving your dreams is like planting a tree. You plant the seed, water it, and nurture it until it has grown. In the end, you want that tree to bare fruit. A good tree produces good fruit; a bad tree produces bad fruit. This is why the idea of making yourself better in order to become a Success Magnet™ is so powerful. If you are the tree that produces the fruit (results) in your life, you should be working on yourself to bring forth the fruit you want. 'Results are the fruits from the seed that you have planted.

You can't plant weeds and expect to get an amazing tree with big juicy fruit on it. That's just how things are on this planet. The law of sowing and reaping says you reap what you sow. On that day that changed my life, I realized I was reaping all those terrible things because of what I had sown in the past.

- *Poor Planning*

Having a plan is absolutely essential to achieving anything. "People who fail to plan, plan to fail" is one of my favorite sayings because planning is what I needed most in my life. When I first decided what I wanted, I didn't have a plan to obtain it, so I was moving in random directions instead of toward my goals. A plan is essentially a map, a map that shows you not only where you are going but also how to get there. If you were dropped off in the middle of Los Angeles, and you'd never been to LA before, and your goal was to make it to the airport, how could you do that without a map? A plan is the same thing: you can't get to your goal destination without a plan. I believe every single value should have goals and plans to achieve those goals. Everyone should have a financial plan, a plan to acquire more wisdom and skills, a plan on how to keep their relationships fresh, a plan on keeping optimal health and fitness, and a plan to cultivate a higher sense of spirituality.

Planning strategically has been all the difference in changing my life. I decide what I want. Then I set a goal to achieve it.

After the day that turned my life around, I became a voracious reader. I noticed in every self-help book I read that the authors all said you must set goals. At first, I just wrote down crazy goals. But in the next few months, my life changed. I had actually achieved some of those crazy goals—and more. I then became a goal-setting student. I read plenty of books, listened to tons of audio programs, and went to several seminars on goal setting. After trying different goal-setting strategies, I finally came up with a system that works for me. I was able to achieve all of my financial, mental, emotional, and spiritual goals in 2013.

– *Lack of Resources*

Lots of people never achieve what they dream of because they claim they lack resources. The two

If you would like to learn my secrets on goal setting, visit my website at www.royredd.com for a free ebook Finish: 7 secrets to achieve your goals.)

most common recourses people claim keep them from trying to achieve anything is lack of time and lack of money. These excuses are far from the actual truth. Plenty of people had less time than you and less money than you but went on to achieve great things. I love Tony Robbins quote" "It's not about your recourses; it's about your resourcefulness." It's not about what you have; it's about what you do with what you have that determines your life. Scripture says, in 2 Corinthians 8, "For if the willingness is there, the gift is acceptable according to what one has, not according to what he does not have" (New International Version). " If you believe in, or have faith in, what you want to accomplish, it will be accepted based on what you have, not what you think you need to have. You can only work with what you have in your current circumstances.

You need two things to break through the wall of lack of time and resources: the mindset it takes to stay consistent and a role model.

MINDSET

Your mindset is, without doubt, the defining factor in achieving what you want in life. You cannot control what happens to you, but you can control what you do about it. We all have problems and obstacles in our life; that's just part of living. The difference is what we decide to do about it. Our actions can be no better than our thinking, and our thinking can be no better than our understanding, so we must understand that we need a successful mindset to succeed. People generally have one of two types of mindsets: a loser's mindset or a winner's mindset.

– *Loser's Mindset*

A person with a loser's mindset is someone who is quick to quit. This person makes excuses why she can't achieve her goals, and she complains about everything. My mother always says to me, "Excuses are for the incompetent, and those who specialize in them will never succeed." These people who make excuses for everything never go anywhere in life. An excuse is a foundation that allows you to stand on something to protect your pride, just in case you never achieve what you want. The way the brain works is when we ask ourselves a question about our life, if we don't like the answer, we either fix it or make an excuse to comfort our pride.

I remember when I was first in EMT school. I was scared of how hard it was. I was so nervous about not making it through that I started to come up with my excuse on why I couldn't make it before I even tried. I remember telling my mother how 30 people started the class, and only 8 passed. And of those 8, 6 were repeats. I was giving my mother my excuses for not passing, just in case I didn't make it through. My mother looked at me and said, "Well, you're not like those people. You are smart, so you better pass that damn class."

My mother is one of those strong individuals who doesn't believe in failure. She strongly believes in getting the job done by any means necessary. She is far from having a victim mindset. So, as I went into the class, I told myself that I was going to do this, no matter how hard it is. And I did.

Another thing people with victim mindsets do is complain all of the time. One way to throw away your future easily is to complain. Complaining will keep you from moving forward because you're wasting your time complaining rather than fixing the problem. When you're on a mission, your worst enemy is idle time, and complaining is idle time at its best.

The Bible talks about the children of Israel and how complaining caused them to be cast away. The children of Israel were slaves, and God performed a bunch of miracles through Moses to help free them from slavery. After they were free from slavery, they had to take a long, hard travel to what was said to be the Promised Land. On their way to the Promised Land, they were short on food and clothes and shelter. God gave them food and all the things they needed to make it. After being freed and having what they needed to make it to the Promised Land, the children of Israel had the nerve to start complaining. They complained about the food. They complained about the long walks. And they complained about the leadership. They complained as if they had completely forgotten that they had just been slaves. They had lost all their gratitude. After years of complaining, God finally had enough and cast them into the city of Babylon instead of their Promised Land.

Don't complain. Come from a place of gratitude because

there is always someone worse off than you. There is a Persian saying: "I cursed not having any shoes until I saw the man with no feet." Things can always be worse. So, as you strive for your success, be gracious with what you have.

Lastly, you must never quit. Quitting because things aren't going your way is the worst thing you can do. Any goal worth achieving will be hard and require lots of persistence. If it were easy and we could achieve your goals the first or second try, then everyone would be successful.

Think of how the world would be if some of our greatest leaders had quit. What if Martin Luther King, Jr., had said "these people don't understand and never will," and had

A quitter never ends up with anything worthwhile in life because anything of any real value takes time, hard work, and consistency.

just quit? How would the world be now if he had never stuck to his goal? What if he had quit and just let his dream die in him and took it to the grave? Where would we be as a society?

– *Winner's Mindset*

A winning mindset is the one that says I'm going to do whatever it takes to get this done. Winners are A players in life. A players are self-starting, not reactive, but proactive, people. These are the people who say, "If I don't have something, or I don't know something, I am going to go get it, or I'm going to learn it." In psychology, they call this the causal agent mindset. A causal agent mindset is one that gives you total control over where your life ends up. People with this mindset believe that everything that happens to them is because of what they did to attract it. These people truly believe in the law of sowing and reaping, and they use the law to their advantage as best they can. These are the people who don't complain when things go bad, and they don't apologize when things go well. These are the people with lots of self-efficacy in their lives.

When I think of a winner's mindset, I think of Benjamin Franklin. We all know Franklin as the man who used a lightning rod to harness electricity. We all know the story about how he flew a kite to attract lightning and prove his theories about electricity. Franklin set the foundation for future scientists to control electricity, just as Thomas Edison did with the light bulb. But what never gets told in the history books is how many times Franklin failed. Before the invention that changed the world, Franklin was considered a kook. Many people criticized and made fun of him for trying thousands of inventions and never succeeding. A man asked Franklin one day, "Why do you keep trying and failing."

"I didn't fail," he replied. "I just found thousands of ways to do it wrong."

To me, that's what a true winner's mindset is. It's an unshakable confidence that he would eventually find the answer. When you set out to achieve something, don't let anything or anyone get into your head to stop you. You must have the resolve to say I'm going to get this done, no matter what happens. Create the winner's mindset you need, and protect it with all of your power, and you will achieve anything you wish for—guaranteed.

4 Things I Ask of You
1. Don't have a loser's mindset. Have a winner's mindset.
2. Never let your dreams die in you.
3. Stop cheating the world of your talents and develop a stick-to-it philosophy that nothing can break.
4. Be great.

GET COACHING

One of the best ways to learn how to achieve the goals you want is to get coaching. There are plenty of people out there who have done what you want to do with less or the same recourses you have. Find these people and learn from them best as you can. When you set your goals in life, think to yourself who has done this and what you can learn from that person to help you. A coach in a mentor that guides you as best as he can to where you want to go.

The most successful people all have had coaches. This is because they understand the importance of guidance and being held accountable. I use to think coaching was a scam to just get people's money when I was ignorant to its benefits.

I attended a seminar that featured some of the world's most successful people. After listening to people speak, and conversing with different people, I noticed they all had coaches.

There's a reason the best singers have a vocal coach: a coach gives them a different view than their own on improvement. This is why after a doctor is done with school, she has to shadow another doctor until she is ready to work alone. They call this residency; but in all honesty, it's just coaching. A professional basketball team does not have one coach but coaches for every skill. There is a head coach, an assistant coach, a shooting coach, a dribbling coach. Each coach is an expert in his specific speciality. What if basketball, football, and baseball teams didn't have coaches? There would be no order, no improvement, and no motivation.

When I finally learned the importance of coaching, the first thing I did was get a coach. Having a coach had a dramatic impact on me achieving my goals. He was able to look at my life and business at a different angle and give me quality input.

The important thing about selecting a coach is finding someone who can help you in the areas you most need help on. If you are reading this book, I am coaching you on the philosophies that helped me get to where I am. Everybody gets coaching; but not everyone 'looks at it from the viewpoint of intentionally finding a coach. Coaches help you take your knowledge, skills, and talents, and organize them. A coach can keep you motivated on your road to achieving what you want in your life or in your business.

Now that we have looked at the common obstacles and how to overcome them, let's get down

"Go to RoyRedd.com to contact Roy for a free coaching call."

to business. In the next chapter, I begin to break down each value and ideas on how to cultivate them best as you can.

THE PERFECT CIRCLE

Circle (n.): a round plane figure whose boundary (the circumference) consists of points equidistant from a fixed point (the center).

Before we dive into the framework for this book, I want to make an important point. I do a lot of reading and studying on different random topics. One day I was reading about the absence of a perfect circle in our universe. Scientists have been attempting to make, and searching for, a perfect circle all throughout the galaxy. They can't make one themselves. There are no planets or structures in the universe that are perfect circles. And there is no machine that can make one. As far as human beings' knowledge up to now, there is no such thing as a perfect circle in the entire universe. When I read the definition of a circle, and realized there isn't one in the entire universe, it mustered up a question in me: why is it that we can define a perfect circle, yet there is no such thing? This opened my eyes to another thought: if we can define a perfect circle, but can't achieve it, maybe other things we define can never be achieved. Socially, we define things and we can never achieve them and wonder why we never feel successful.

Humans have a natural need for growth, so we set ideals for ourselves and then base our success on the fact of if we reach that ideal or not. When you set out to set goals and cultivate your values to succeed, do not make your goals the ideal of society. It is important to make your own personal ideals. Do not define success based on what society says it is, but define what success is for you. Remember, there is no such thing as a perfect circle, even if you can define it.

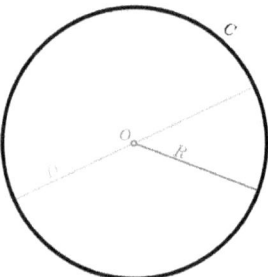

Even on this diagram the circle is not perfect.

CHAPTER 4

BUILD A FINANCIAL WALL NOTHING CAN BREAK

FINANCIAL FREEDOM

Financial freedom is, in my opinion, something everyone should strive for. Financial freedom is having the ability to live off your past efforts. Being financially free allows you to live life in the way you wish without worry or stress. I believe financial freedom is a worthwhile goal that everyone should have for themselves. Being financially free releases you from being a slave to being a lender. The Bible says, "The rich rule over the poor, and the borrower is slave to the lender" (Proverbs 22:7, NIV).

Financial freedom is the process by which you set yourself up so that you are no longer a borrower. It allows you to be free of the lenders of the world so that you can bring to pass all of your dreams and ambitions. Financial freedom is not as hard to accomplish as you think. Although I am not financially free yet, I have a plan that will bring me to that goal in a matter of time. Most people have no idea how to allocate their finances in the proper way. In the first five years of my working life, I was the same way. This is why when I got in a pinch, I had nothing in the bank, no money to my name to help myself get out of trouble.

I remember a truck that my parents bought me when I was 16 years old. I drove that truck for seven years until the engine went out. Because I didn't save my money the way I should have, I ended up not having the money to fix my truck and had to sell it. That's how I ended up with the beat-up vehicle I talked about in prior chapters. There was no reason I shouldn't have had the money I needed to fix my truck, and it would have taken me another strong seven years. But when I look back at it, if I hadn't lost that truck and went through what I did, I wouldn't have learned what I needed to know to move toward the financial freedom I want. If you follow the plan and ideas I'm going to share with you, you will be financially free within 20 years—or sooner if you find a good opportunity. Build a financial wall around your family that nothing can break. It's simpler than you think.

MORE MINDSETS

– The Poor Man's Mindset

First thing we have to talk about is the mindset it takes to become as financially free as we want. A lot of people have a certain mindset, or limiting belief, about money that keeps them from accumulating it. As I talk about some of these poor mindsets, I want you to take a real look at yourself and ask yourself, do I have any of these poor mindsets?

– *The Money-Is-Evil Mindset*

Some people have a limiting belief that money is the root of all evil. They think that they need to just be grateful for what they have and never strive for too much. They believe that trying to make more money is being greedy, and being greedy means that you love money. These beliefs could 'not be further from the truth. Money is just a by-product of value created. It is only a person's hard work and time put into material form. For example: if you make $20 an hour, all a 20-dollar bill is, is a hour of your time, or the value of an hour of your time.

I believe we should all be grateful for what we have as we strive for more. There is nothing wrong with money. The Bible says,

> "For the love of money is a root of all kinds of evil. Some people, eager for money, have wandered from the faith and pierced themselves with many griefs" (1 Timothy 6:10, NIV).

This means loving money is evil, not that money is evil itself.

Let's say you earn your living in a job that you love. You are creating value doing what you love to do. Money is just the result of doing what you love. Does that make money evil?

In one of my favorite books of all time, Atlas Shrugged, by Ayn Rand, a scene comes to mind. One of the characters, Francisco D'aconia, is extremely rich.' Francisco is attending a party, and during a conversation, someone" says that money is the root of all evil." This is what Francisco has to say:

> So you think money is the root of all evil? Have you ever asked what is the root of money? Money is a tool of exchange, which can't exist unless there are goods produced and men to produce them. Money is the material shape of the principle that men who wish to deal with one another must deal by trade and give value for value. Money is not the tool of the moochers, who claim your product by tears, or the looters, who take it from you by force. Money is made possible only by the men who produce. Is this what you consider evil?

When I first read this, it changed my whole outlook on money. It made me realize that money is only a tool of exchange that represents what I had worked for. Money is not evil; it is actually good in every way. Money represents a material achievement of the individual. It represents your productivity and the application of your mind to achieve results. Money is not evil in any shape or form. Money is a value.

– *The Material Mindset*

This is a mindset I struggled with in the past and still struggle with today. The material mindset is the mindset of people who always buy nice things and keep up with the latest. We all want to have the latest things that make us look, as though we were ahead of the game. People do a great job of managing material things because it makes them feel good to have the latest. The problem with this is it doesn't last. No matter what you buy, there will always be something else you want and think you need to have.

I like nice clothes and shoes. At one point in my life, I had to have the latest Nikes whenever they came out. I was spending anywhere from a $100 to $300, just for some dumb shoes that made me feel good. The problem is that feeling only lasts for a little while. You have to get the next pair of shoes that comes out the next week. It's a never-ending cycle.

Will Durant said, "The men who can manage men manage the men who only manage things, and the men who can manage money manage all." Instead of trying to manage all the material things of the world, learn to manage your money. That's true freedom. Don't become a slave to the material things of this world. We all know intellectually that all the things we buy 'don't bring us any true value in the long run, but we still have a shopping problem. Let me tell you why this is.

Our bodies releases a hormone called serotonin when we feel a since of pride or status. Serotonin is the leadership hormone. Serotonin makes a stronger connection between the leader and the people being led, between parent and child, between teacher and student, between coach and player.

An example of how serotonin works: Graduating high school isn't difficult at all. All you really have to do is go to class, do a little work, and in four years gather a diploma. But instead of the school just giving you a diploma, it throws you a big celebration called a graduation. The reason for this is serotonin. When you go across that stage and grab your diploma, you get a big surge of serotonin, and you feel pride and status. The cool part about serotonin is that at the very same moment you get that surge of serotonin, your parents in the audience get the same surge of serotonin. This makes them feel proud of you and happy for you. This is why when people go up to get an award, when they give their speech, they say things like, "I could not have done this without my parents." That's serotonin at its best.

The problem with serotonin is we can trick ourselves into getting this hormone through material things. Since we live in a materialistic society, the way to feel pride and status is based on how much money we have. So, people buy the nice cars, the nice clothes, or the latest gadgets to show people how well they're doing. This is why we wear the high-end clothes so that everybody can see us. It makes us feel like we are walking across that stage again getting our diploma—but we really aren't. When I purchased those new Nikes and wore them, I felt I had high status, and I wanted the compliments on my shoes.

This is also why we share our successes on social networks. We do something we are proud of and we post it on Instagram and Facebook, and every time we get a "like," we get a dose of serotonin. Some people, literally, post a picture of their new expensive shoes, and they watch their pages like a hawk, refreshing them every second to see how many "likes" they can get. It's not because they are materialistic; it's because they want that sense of pride and status—they want the serotonin.

– The Rich Man's Mindset

People who are finically free, or rich, think in a different way than most. They have developed a better way of thinking that has allowed them to accumulate and save money the way it should be done. If you want to be financially free, start with the right mindset to set up the disciplines it will take to achieve financial freedom. The rich man's mindset comes down to a couple of, what I call, submindsets.

– Happy Taxpayer

One submindset rich people have pertains to how they think about taxes. Having a happy taxpayer's mindset means you know the importance of paying your taxes. Right now you might be thinking, "Wait, rich people hate paying their taxes."

Look at what I just wrote: "Having a happy taxpayer's mindset means you know the importance of paying your taxes."

We all must pay taxes, no matter how high we think they might be. We live in a beautiful utopia of enterprise and freedom to do or become whatever we wish. None of this is free. The roads we use, the police and firefighters, the postal system, and all the things we take for granted are not free. Somebody has to pay for all of this to be possible. Jesus said:

> "Give back to Caesar what is Caesar's and to
> God what is God's" (Mark 12:17, NIV).

Caesar was the emperor of Rome at the time and had issued a tax everybody had to pay.

Once while visiting the temple, one of Jesus's disciples came to him and said they didn't have the money to pay the temple tax. Jesus said,

> But so that we may not offend them, go to the
> lake and throw out your line. Take the first
> fish you catch; open its mouth and you will
> find a four-drachma coin. Take it and give
> it to them for my tax and yours. (Matthew
> 17:27, NIV)

Now, that was easy for this disciple to do because his name was Peter, and Peter was a fisherman. Peter went fish-ing. When he caught his first fish, he looked in the fish's mouth and there were coins. There were enough coins to pay his taxes and Jesus's taxes. So if Jesus and Peter paid taxes without complaint, I think we should all pay our taxes without complaint as well.

You can say that the government uses our money in bad ways. But if you think about it, we all use money wrong sometimes. You can say the president uses our money recklessly. But we all spend money a little recklessly sometimes. We have to have a society, we have to have a government, or we couldn't have any marketplace that allows us to prosper. But after you pay your taxes, what should you do with your money?

THE ARKAD PLAN

One of my favorite books of all time—the book that taught me how to allocate my money—is The Richest Man in Babylon. The Richest Man in Babylon, written by George Clason, is a parable about a man named Arkad who became the richest man in the richest city in the world. Babylon is said to be the first city to exchange money for goods and services. Babylon was a lot like the world we live in today. It had a lower class, a middle class, and an upper class.

Arkad was part of the lower class. He made a living working as a scribe. He started to build ambition for more in his life. He started to ask himself questions about why some people were rich and some people were poor. He wasn't sure if it was just plain luck or if there was some sort of secret to accumulating wealth.

One day a very wealthy man named Algamish came to Arkad looking to have a law inscribed on a clay tablet. Arkad asked Algamish how he was able to become rich and what was his secret. They ended up making a deal: if Arkad would scribe for Algamish, he would, in return, give him the secrets of wealth. Arkad worked hard and all through the night to finish the inscription. The next morning when Algamish came to retrieve the inscription, it was ready and nicely done. Algamish was a man of his word, so he told Arkad the secret of wealth. He told him that what he was about to tell him was not going to be as groundbreaking as Arkad had thought, but if he understood this, he could have all the wealth he wanted. He said, "A part of what I earn is mine to keep."

– A Part of What I Earn Is Mine to Keep

Algamish told Arkad to keep at least 10 percent of his earnings. He said save this 10 percent before you pay your bills or buy clothes or food. Arkad believed what Algamish said, so he saved a 10th of his earnings for a whole year.

After 12 months went by, Algamish came back to check on Arkad and asked about his savings and what he has done with it. Arkad told him that he had saved up a good amount of earnings, and he gave it to a brickmaker who was going to a far land to purchase jewels. Algamish laughed at him and said, "Every fool must learn." He " asked Arkad why he would trust the knowledge of a brickmaker about jewels"" and why would he take advice about his own savings from someone who is not experienced in this matter? He told Arkad to consider that money gone and to start over.

Another year went by, and Arkad had saved up his money again. Algamish came by to check on Arkad and his savings as he did the year prior. Arkad had saved at least a 10th of his earrings again, and this time he invested in a shieldmaker who needed materials to make his products. Every fourth month the shieldmaker paid Arkad interest on the money he landed making the shields. Algamish asked Arkad what he did with the money he got from the shieldmaker? Arkad told him he used the earnings for clothing and regularly scheduled feasts. Algamish told Arkad he was eating the children of his savings by not investing them.

Finally, Arkad became as wise as he wanted to be. He adjusted his behavior and started to apply all of the lessons Algamish taught him. Algamish was a great coach to Arkad.

After two more years went by, Algamish visited Arkad and was proud of the improvements he had made. Algamish was getting old and didn't want to leave his estate to someone who couldn't handle it in the proper way, so he decided to leave it to Arkad. Arkad grew to become the richest man in Babylon.

– *Pay Yourself First*

All the people that I have met that are well off financially pay themselves first. When they get their check, and taxes are already taken out, they immediately pay themselves before they pay bills or buy anything. Paying yourself first is the golden rule of all finances. Take 10 percent of everything you earn and save it. Have it automatically taken out of your check and put into an account that you cannot see or touch. This is a great way to discipline yourself to save. Money you don't see is money you forget about. This money grows slowly, but it's well worth it later.

Then what you do with this money you have saved is invest it. Invest it in a company or companies that borrow your money to make more. They then, in turn, pay you a percentage of interest on the money you let them borrow. Remember, the borrower is servant to the lender. This is an amazing way to put yourself in the position of the lender.

− *Make a Profit*

Save another 10 percent of your income to make a profit. Use another 10 percent of your income to use toward ideas, business, or an opportunity. Take this 10 percent and figure out ways to make profits with this money. Profits are better than wages. Jim Rohn said, "Wages will make you a living, but profits can make you a fortune."

When I first learned of the idea of saving 10 percent of my income for profits, I began to save but had no clue for what. I had no clue how to make a profit with this money, but I saved it anyway. Then one day I got the idea of opening my own CPR business. I looked into it and found it would cost me around $3000 to get started. I had the money I needed because I had started to save money to make a profit or start a business. I was able to double my income rapidly just by starting this small business. When I made just as much in my business as I did at my job, it opened my eyes to entrepreneurship. We all can't just up and start a business. Not all of us have the money. But if you save part of your income for this purpose, you can start to accumulate it and build a business in no time.

Have you ever had ambitions to start a small business or had a great opportunity that required money but you couldn't invest because you had no money? That's the primary reason for this 10 percent to be saved. It puts you in a position to play your cards when a good hand is dealt to you.

− Give

With the last 10 percent of your money that you allocate, give it away. Some call it paying their tides, and some just give to those who can't help themselves.

There is the story about the 12 disciples standing watching people pay their tides. Many people came and paid different amounts. Jesus sat down opposite the place where the

Giving is one of the most amazing things you can do. To give to help someone, not to get anything back, makes you feel so good.

offerings were put and watched the crowed putting its money into the temple treasury. Many rich people threw in large amounts. A poor widow came and put in two very small pieces of copper coins, worth only a fraction of a penny. Jesus called his disciples to him:

> Truly I tell you, he said, this poor widow has put in more than all the others. All these people gave their gifts out of their wealth; but she out of her poverty put in all she had to live on. (Luke 21:3–4, NIV)

Giving is the most important thing anyone can do in life. When I can help someone—just because I want to and not for any personal gain—it feels so amazing.

How you think about giving is the most important part. Don't give to get. That's selfish. But rather give because it's the right thing to do. When you give to others, the universe, God, or nature—whatever you believe in—will naturally reciprocate. Giving that comes from a mind of generosity actually feels good. There is a reason for this. (We will visit later in the book why it feels so great when we talk about cultivating the value of love.)

THE TWO ECONOMIES

Generally, most people are completely clueless to the fact that there is more than one economy. Most people think that the economy consists of the time and effort they put in. Usually, these people have jobs and only see their money-stream coming from the time and effort they put in that job. But the time-and-effort economy is not scaleable. No matter how much effort you put into a job, you get paid the same. This is why every company has people who suck at their job, people who are average at their job, and people who are good at their job. This is because they all are paid the same way regardless of the value they bring. Some people are extremely lucky and get paid at their job equivalent to the results they bring. This brings us to the second economy.

This second economy is the results economy, which means you get paid for the results you produce. When people get paid based on results, they tend to work harder and smarter. Some people are in this results economy and don't even know they are in this type of system.

I learned of the results economy after I started a small CPR business. When I realized I had doubled my income just by teaching small CPR classes, it changed my whole outlook on making money. I realized I was working with way less effort than I did in my day job, but I was making just as much money. I had discovered the results economy, and it required less time and less effort.

Even though the results economy is much easier and pays much more, there is one main reason people don't start their own business: risk. Most people don't step into the results economy because of the amount of risk it takes. The results economy is easier, frees up more time, and pays better—but it's risky. When you come to the door that leads to the results economy, you have to pay the price of security to get in. This is why it kills me when people complain about the rich getting taxed more just because they make more money. They make more money because they take more risks. You can't have the security of your job and expect to have the opportunity that the wealthy have. If you took a huge risk and you happened to become wealthy, how would you feel if someone wanted more of your money? If you read books about these wealthy people, most of them gave up the security of their job and went bankrupt trying to start businesses. They stepped out on faith and were rewarded for that faith in the long run. We all have a choice: we can have a secure job or we can take the risk to achieve our dreams.

MONEY DOES BUY HAPPINESS

Most people tell you that money can't buy you happiness. These people either don't have money or don't want to seem materialistic. When people tell me money doesn't buy happiness, I usually respond by saying, "That's because you don't know where to shop." Money is totally OK to have, and if used properly, can by all the happiness in the world. Let's visit the three levels of happiness that money can buy.

– *Happiness Level 1*

First off when we think about money, we usually think

about all of the things we can buy. All of the boats, cars, homes, that we value and dream about having. There is nothing wrong with having the biggest, most beautiful things money can buy. But before you buy them, I want you to know that they make you only just a little bit happy, and for a short amount of time. When we buy these things, it is important to realize that we are actually paying for an experience—nothing more, nothing less. When we spend money on experiences, they can give us a certain level of happiness.

It seems to me that we are here on earth to achieve as much knowledge as possible. When we think of knowledge, we, for the most part, think of information. Knowledge is not just information; it is also applying that information so that you attain true knowledge. The root word of knowledge is know for a good reason. When you know something with absolute certainty, then you have knowledge, and you cannot know anything until you have achieved and experienced it. We can believe that a time machine is possible, but we won't know it is possible until someone builds it and travels in time. With this truth, it is safe to say that through the pursuit of knowledge, we humans desire experiences. This is why material things bring us happiness: the clothes, the cars, the big home, the vacations give us an experience. What's the difference between a Bentley and a Honda Civic? They both have the same function. They both have the means to get you from one place to another place. The Bentley is more valuable because it provides an experience

When you have lived an experience and you have obtained the knowledge that comes from the experience, you will no longer get any happiness from that experience.

that a Honda can't. So, it's important to know the difference between what we need and what makes us feel good. And that difference is the experience we receive. Humans live to grow and perpetuate as many experiences as they possibly can so that they can become as knowledgeable as they possibly can. Through experience comes knowledge, so we desire a huge amount of experience.

– *Happiness Level 2*

When someone tells you that money can't buy happiness, it is because they are only aware of the fact that experiences don't bring lasting happiness. They are not aware of the fact that there are other things to purchase that bring happiness, like the next one we will talk about.

We also can purchase time with money. Studies have shown when money is used to get rid of transactional tasks—like cleaning, laundry, or anything that takes up our time—our happiness goes up considerably and lasts. Imagine how happy your life would be if you could spend all of your time on only what you want to spend your time on. If that wouldn't make you happy, then I don't know what would. Time is something we can never get back, which makes it much more valuable than money. When we can free up our time, our happiness goes to the ceiling. But the next thing that money can buy will make your happiness go through the roof.

I'm sitting having lunch with a good friend who is a multimillionaire and a mentor to me. I had invited this person to lunch when I first met him to pick his brain. If you want to have great value and ideas dropped in your lap, invite a wealthy person to lunch. This guy drops a lot of ideas, secrets, and motivation in my lap in just an hour's time. After the lunch is over and the waitress brings us the bill, I gladly grab the bill to pay it.

As I do, this gentlemen grabs my hand, looks me in the eye, and says, "Are you that selfish, so selfish you're going to rob me of the great feeling I would get if I pay for your lunch?"

I'm so confused. I just want to pay for lunch, especially after he has just changed my life with his knowledge. He then smiles, and the lunch goes on another hour while he explains to me what he was referring to. He knows what to spend his money on. He is truly a guy who knows how to buy happiness.

– *Happiness Level 3*

Lastly, and most importantly, money can buy us extreme happiness when we spend it on other people. We all know the feeling we get when we are able to spend money on family, friends, and even strangers. Even if it's a few dollars, we feel amazing after spending money on someone else. To prove it, all you have to do is juxtapose your happiness when you bought yourself something expensive, and when you gave away only a dollar to a person in need. We get much more of a sense of happiness and fulfillment when we give to others than when we give to ourselves. If you want happiness, earn enough money to treat yourself, buy back your time, and give money to others to achieve their outcomes. Money spent properly—yes, indeed—can buy happiness.

MONEY AND VALUE

Value (n.): the size of the problems you can solve.

Now that we have talked about how to allocate money, let's talk about how to make it. People who 'don't understand how the marketplace works believe that hard work on a good job is what makes more money. In turn, they believe they need a good degree to get that good job. The marketplace does not care how hard you work or what your degree is in. The marketplace cares only about the value you bring to it. The bigger the problem a company or a person or the marketplace has, the more it will pay to have it fixed.

If you can go into a company and teach the leaders in an hour's time something that will allow them to make a million dollars more than they have, will they pay you

$100,000 for that hour? Of course they will because in the long run, they are going to be able to make much more money based off your knowledge.

Another way to bring value is to fix everyday life problems. One way to do this is to know what to listen for. When you hear someone say they hate something, usually that's an indicator of a problem that can be fixed.

I was watching a commercial about a water hose that doesn't get kinks in it because of how it is made. I absolutely hate it when the water hose gets kinks in it when I'm washing my car. My next thought was, "Why didn't I come up with that idea; it seems really simple." The truth is it is simple, and it solves an everyday problem.

The marketplace is a tree to climb. The tree starts at the roots, also known as minimum wage. The top of the tree is where Warren Buffet is, making $37 million a day in 2013. Now, how did he go from minimum wage to making $37 million a day? He became more valuable by being able to solve major problems in the marketplace.

2 Ways to Get Higher up the Marketplace Tree

1. Jump on the tree by getting a job and waiting for the tree to grow. The problem with waiting on the tree to grow is as the tree grows, so do expenses. So, really, you remain in the same place.
2. Climb the tree. And the only way to

climb this hell of a tree is to become
more valuable.

One thing we must remember is that we don't get paid
for time. Don't make the mistake of thinking you make a
certain amount of money per hour. The money you make is
only the value you put into the hour. The secret to bringing
more value to the marketplace is working on yourself. You
can't chase money; it will allude you. You must make yourself a Success Magnet™ by becoming more valuable to the
marketplace. When you become more valuable, money will
come to you with ease.

– *Ideas*

Another way to bring value to the marketplace is with
great ideas. One good idea can literally change the world.

In 2004, Mark Zuckerberg had this amazing idea to use
the Internet as a social network for students. He realized
the importance of people wanting to know what others were
doing, and connecting all of us through the Internet. So,
he started Facebook. Facebook took the world by storm.
Today, Mark is the youngest billionaire in the world after
starting a business worth $106 billion.

When it comes to ideas, all you have to do is get a lot
of people to believe in your idea. I call it ideas that affect
the many". The law of affection states that the more people you can affect in an entity that you control by scale or

magnitude, the more money you will make. The formula is easy: come up with a good idea and act on it, and you will accumulate money in an abundance you never thought of. So, if all you need to do is come up with a good idea, how are ideas cultivated? (We will talk about that later when we get to the cultivation of wisdom.)

Ideas come from a constant intake of information. Ideas also come from paying attention to everything. If you lack anything, it's not money; it's ideas to make money.

Another way to use ideas to make money is to borrow ideas and articulate them in a different way, or make them better. Steve Jobs didn't invent the computer, but he found ways to improve it and present it in an amazing way. You don't necessarily have to be the creator of an idea, but you can improve old ideas in a way that makes them pertinent for the times.

– *The Drive for Control*

Control is the first human drive. If we don't feel in control of our life, we will never venture out to progress. When we don't feel in control and comfortable, we put ourselves in a cage. The caged self feels limited by external conditions. The urge to control and influence our overall life experiences is what the human drive is all about.

I say this because money is one thing that determines the control in our life. If we don't even know if we can pay our bills or eat, we won't be able to cultivate the other val-

Money is the least important of all values. But you must have it to feel in control enough to work on the others.

ues. This is why money is the first value I talk about. It's the foundation to make you feel safe enough to get the important things done.

As George Clason wrote in The Richest Man in Babylon, "The man who has nothing in his purse is unkind to his family and disloyal, for his own heart is bitter." I've been in that place. The only way to get out of it is by having money. After money was out of the way, I was able to live, love, and try to make a difference in my life and others' lives. I want the same for you. So, even if you don't follow my plan, at least make a plan and cultivate the value of money.

– *Responsibility Makes You Money*

We live in a society where responsibility is a rare character trait. Sadly, people don't wish to take responsibility for anything. We always have excuses for everything. Excuses allow us to protect our identity by blaming circumstance. We sell independence, but we breed dependence. Success Magnets™ are the people who don't allow circumstance to dictate the outcome they want.

I have never met anyone who is just late. What I mean by "just late" is no excuses, no reasons, but just late. When I was late to work, my boss always wanted to know why. I never had an excuse. "I am late because I am late." I might have been late because my tire was flat, traffic was heavy, or I had family problems. The reasons do not matter. The only thing that matters is the outcome. Knowing that, I didn't share the reason because I knew it didn't matter. People don't understand that. My boss always wanted a reason to why I was late. She didn't get that the reason made no difference. The only thing that mattered was that I was late.

This is one of the hardest lessons to learn in becoming self-efficient. It's hard when you don't come through to just own up to it. But a true leader takes responsibility. The best leaders not only take responsibility for their own actions but also take responsibility for other people's. The best leaders are also the best paid. Let me tell you why.

It bothered me for a while that people don't take responsibility. You will find that when you develop self-efficacy in your life, you will separate from a lot of friends. They will not understand you when you try to articulate that their excuses don't matter. One day I was thinking about this when a light bulb went on in my head. If people don't take responsibility, maybe I can use that to my advantage to make money. People will pay me tons of money to take the responsibility they are scared of taking. Think about it. People pay trainers, doctors, accountants, lawyers, and insurance companies because they don't want the responsibility for their own health, fitness, and money. They choose to pay others and give them the responsibility. If they succeed, they are a genius for hiring that person. If things go bad, they have their much-needed excuse: "My doctor is an idiot. My trainer is bad. My accountant ruined me. My lawyer 'lost my case."

With this new information, all you have to do is take the responsibility for them and they will pay you. At a job, take responsibility for all your work and other people's work, and see the response you get. In business, articulate your marketing in a way that you invite your prospects to give the responsibility to you, and see what happens. Most people love to follow authority figures and people with positions because it rids them of their own responsibility. (Later we will see a little more deeply why people follow authority figures.)

– *Responsibility Saves You Money*

That people don't want responsibility is well known to the world's top marketers. These marketers and companies use this fact to their advantage. Some might have good products and services, and some might not; regardless, they market in the form of asking you for your responsibility, and most people fall for the trap. That's what a guarantee is. A promise in the form of a guarantee is just a smarter way of saying I'll take responsibility for your outcome for you.

Never put your values in the hands of anyone else—never! It's OK to receive counsel, but always decide for yourself. If the decision ends up being the wrong decision, it's OK. That's a learning experience for you. But don't let someone else learn what or what not to do with your money, your health, your learning, or your spirituality. The question you should ask yourself is, am I giving up my self-efficacy by paying for this product? If you are, you must give it a lot of consideration whether you want to purchase it or not. You can save tons of money by just taking responsibility and getting the information yourself. When you put the responsibility in others' hands, you feel hopeless and lack self-efficacy. Take full 100 percent responsibility for everything in your world—period.

– *Money and Success*

The biggest reason people have the wrong view on success is they believe they need more money to be successful. Remember, success is the attainment of a future ideal; it has nothing to do with how much money you make. Money is the by-product of the success. You're not successful when you have money—money comes from being successful. Most people have it backwards. They believe they aren't successful because they don't have the amount of money that society says makes you a success. But money comes after you are already successful. So, the key is to achieve the ideal you have for yourself, and the money will come on its own. You don't make money, unless you work at the U.S. Treasury. We earn it. You earn money by bringing value to the marketplace. The value you bring is the ideal you have for your life. When you bring that ideal to the marketplace, you are now successful. The marketplace pays you for your success. So, focus on being successful by becoming who you want to be, and the money will appear in congruence with the person you have become. This is the key to becoming a Success Magnet™.

CHAPTER 5

GAIN EXPERIENCE, ATTAIN KNOWLEDGE, USE GOOD JUDGMENT

INVEST YOUR PAST

Wisdom comes from having the experience to know what worked or did not work in the past, having the knowledge and information to achieve what you wish, and being able to make the right decisions moving forward in life. To have the experience that wisdom requires comes with time, obviously. The problem is people let this time go to waste. I hear people say frequently to forget about your past. That's a terrible philosophy in my opinion. Your past is the body of work that gives you the ability to make better judgments in the future. When my friends have a birthday, I always tell them, "Take your past, and invest it into your great future." This statement has so much value if you really think about it.

When we were kids, we all had that moment when our mother or father told us "not to touch the hot stove'." We didn't listen. We touched the stove, and it burned us. At that point, we decided not to touch the stove anymore because we did not wish to be burned again. This is what investing your past for your future is. There are certain things in life you have to know; if you don't know, you can get hurt. And if these things hurt you and you continue to do them, guess what? They are going to hurt you again and again. This is why I carry a journal. I capture different life experiences that are good or bad so I know what to do in the future. I've had to learn this lesson the hard way over and over again.

In my early years of working, I made pretty good money for someone my age. My problem was I never saved any money. I spent it all soon as I got it. I would struggle for at least three days for gas and food until I got my next check. I did this for years, not learning my lesson, until one day I had absolutely nothing. Why is it that we do this destructive behavior to ourselves knowing it's not what's best for us? If you do not learn your lesson, nature or God or whatever you believe in has a funny way of teaching you the lesson. The key is to not be like I was; instead, be proactive.

I was asking God for more. But why would He give me more if I didn't know what to do with it? So, He gave me a blessing in a different way. He forced me to learn through my struggles. I'm so glad it happened because it taught me the lessons I needed to know.

> *Proactive people are self-starting people who don't need a really bad situation to teach them the lessons they need to know.*

Another illustration of this is in bad relationships. Let's say your boyfriend has cheated on you. Yet you decide to stay with him and give him another chance. If someone cheats once, he will cheat again. One day he will learn. But he is not going to learn by being rewarded. And you are rewarding him by staying with him.

For human beings, it's detrimental to be rewarded for average or bad behavior. You never reward average or bad behavior. You reward only better-than-average or great behavior. This is why celebrities like Lindsey Lohan continue to live life incongruent with her values. When Lindsey first went to jail and got out, she received a million-dollar deal for an interview the same week. Rewarding her for going to jail engraves a belief into her brain that it's OK to do what she did. So, I'm asking you not to be that person and to follow these simple ideas in this book to become a Success Magnet™, wherever you are in life. "Take your past and invest it into your great future.

There' are two ways we learn. One is insight, and the other is what I call "outsight." The idea of using your past and investing it into the future is insight. It's taking the things you did wrong, and the things you did right, and making future decisions based on those past results. "

OUTSIGHT

Outsight is basically the opposite of insight. You can learn from your experiences, but you can also learn from other people's experiences. The way to do that is to read, listen to instructional audio programs, and take classes that pertain to your goals. When I first got word of an author named Jim Rohn, I literally bought all of his books, all of his audio programs, and all of his DVD programs. If he were still alive today, I would attend all of his seminars. I would listen to this very successful man, who, till this day, is my favorite business philosopher ever. He literally changed the way I think and inspired me to want to be great. As I read and listened to him, I developed this fire in my belly to be successful. This man was everything I wanted to be, so I listened and I read, and I applied his experiences to my life best as I could.

This is the idea of learning from other people. The first way you can learn is by reading books. Did you know thousands of people who were successful (Success Magnets™) wrote books on how they did it, and people have the nerve not to read them? I owe every last bit of success I have to reading books. Anything you wish to be, do, or have in life is first a study. Then it is a practice. Even with something as generic as happiness. Happiness isn't something that just happens. It is first a study on how to be happy, and it is a practice from what you learned. A good book can shave years off your learning curve.

I have a good friend of mine named Trent. Trent is one of those guys who is superambitious, so ambitious he will do anything it takes to achieve his goals. I believe he will achieve his goals because if you search, you shall find. Anyway, Trent told me one day that he wanted to learn stocks. I told him the importance of reading, and so he read one book on stocks. He texted me a week later. "You were right about this reading stuff," he wrote. "I learned so much from just one book that I'm going to read every day."

Reading 'is not only great for learning' but also great for the soul. Jesus said, "It is written: 'Man shall not live on bread alone, but on every word that comes from the mouth of God'" (Matthew 4:4, NIV). Jim Rohn said, "Words nourish the mind, words nourish the soul."

There is absolutely no excuse for not knowing something in our society. All you have to do is grab a good book on the topic. Did you know that certain books are banned in other countries and in jails? The reason for this is because knowledge is extremely powerful if applied. And this knowledge is in books on how to be rich and powerful and persuasive. A lot of these books are so powerful countries don't allow their citizens to read them.

The Bible is a book I read every day, not just because of my religion but also because it teaches me how to live. The Bible is so amazing because it has a bunch of stories that illustrate what's right and what's wrong. It has success stories as well as failure stories. This is awesome because you need to know about both. You need to know what to do as well as what not to do. The Bible is just as practical as it is spiritual. The key is to learn from these outsights and apply them to our lives.

Another way to learn is by listening to what people have to say. You can do this by going to hear a speaker or listening to audio programs. What you listen to, as well as what you read, puts things into your mind. And what you put into your mind comes out in your life. If I'm not in the car with friends, I listen to inspirational audio programs to feed my mind great value. Studies have shown that listening to instructional programs while driving dramatically increases your learning. Based on how much the average person drives, a person can learn up to a bachelor's degree in information in the same amount of time it takes to get the degree. Known as university on wheels, you can get the same amount of education as a full-time student can just by listening to instructional programs while driving. Imagine applying this discipline to your life. Imagine how knowledgeable and how broad your perspective could become. So, set some sort of discipline that allows you to learn from listening as well as reading. If you don't want to listen while driving, allocate some time in your day to sit down and listen.

This is where ideas are born. Ideas come from a constant intake of information. So, if ideas are born from a constant intake of information, naturally, you have to be careful what information you're putting into your head. Listening to programs can resonate with you in a way that could give you ideas on how to improve your life. The information is there; it's everywhere. We just have to be smart enough to take advantage of it. I don't know about you, but this idea excites me so much because I know the importance of cultivating wisdom!

GUARD YOUR MIND

You have to be cautious of what you put into your mind. What you listen to has a dramatic effect on what you sow in life. Jim Rohn said it better than I ever could, "Stand guard at the door of your mind." You can't just walk through life letting anything into your mind because you have to live with the outcome. Search for knowledge and broaden your perspective, but don't assume everything you learn is right. Don't be a follower; be a learner. Be mindful of everything you learn. Question it. Ponder it. Then decide. If you learn about investing from an investor, don't just invest as he says before thinking about it. Seek the counsel of others, but make your own decisions. Even as you read this book, question what 'I'm saying. Ask yourself, does this idea of attracting success instead of chasing it make sense? Remember, everything is opinion based, even though results do speak loudly.

Taking classes is another excellent way to learn. By taking classes, I don't mean school unless the school offers classes that could benefit your purpose. By classes, I mean seminars and workshops taught by someone who has achieved the results you want. If you had to choose between taking a writing class at a school or taking a writing class from a best-selling author, which would you choose? The whole point of learning is to shorten your learning curve. You want to go from A to Z in the fastest way possible. This is why I read, why I listen to audio programs, why I go to seminars, and why I get coaching. I read books from authors who talk about how they have accomplished things. I listen to inspiration programs that keep me vibrant and ready to take on life. I attend seminars given by the best people in the world in their field. And I get coaching from someone who can give me a different perspective on my goals. This is why teachers don't make as much money as other professionals.

People often say our teachers don't make enough even though they are teaching our youth, which is true, but there is a reason for this. If you understand the marketplace, you know that teachers aren't very valuable to the marketplace because they teach theory. They give you the big picture instead of teaching you exactly what to do and why to do it. Not everybody wants to know everything about every subject in school. Those classes are just there as part of the curriculum. If 'there is a subject that you are interested in and want to move forward in, you actually pay attention and get an A grade. But when it's a class you don't care about, you do just enough to get by. And you don't remember any of it when you're done. So, I propose taking classes from the experts in the field you wish to learn. Somebody who has done what you want to do in life can tell you exactly what to do to get there and what obstacles you're going to face.

It took me six years to figure out these small ideas I'm sharing. If you get these ideas, it can shave those six years off your learning curve. The average psychologist makes around $200,000 in the United States, which is good money, by the way. But there is a man by the name of Anthony Robbins, who has no degree in psychology, yet is worth $500 million. The reason for this is simple. A psychologist uses what he learned in a few years of school to help people best as he can. Tony Robbins has been studying psychology his whole life and is known for getting results from the people he coaches every time. If you had to choose to go to a psychologist who might help you or go to Tony and pay more but actually get help moving forward, which would you choose? So, find the learning opportunities that will directly help your purpose, shorten your learning curve, and teach you best practices.

CAPTURE IT

Doesn't matter how much you read, listen, or think if you don't capture what you have learned. You have to capture all the ideas and insights you have from what you learn. Your mind is not a filing cabinet; your mind is for thinking and solving problems. This is why everywhere you go you should keep a journal with you. When you read something good or listen to something motivational or have an original idea, write it down in your journal. In the medical field, we have this saying: "If you didn't chart it, it didn't happen." You can't retain all this information in your head; you have to record it.

Think about how valuable a picture is. A picture says a thousand words. A pictures is the capturing of a moment.

We capture moments so that we can go back and revisit that moment. Have you ever been going through some old pictures and saw a picture you had forgotten about? When you see that picture, you start to bring back memories. You actually replay that whole scene in your head. Capturing something then revisiting it later is like pulling a file from your brain. If you don't capture the moment or the idea, you never filed it away. When you read something that works, write it down. When you hear something that touches you, write it down. When you have an insight on something, write it down. You never know when you might have a random great idea pop into your head, so make sure you keep your journal with you—and write it down.

Imagine if throughout history, nobody had captured the events. We wouldn't have any clue what happened in the past. The Bible wouldn't have been written or any history books that teach us about our past. Our forefathers understood the importance of capturing the moment and the ideas. They understood the importance of their ideas and their perspective on how things happened. So, I'm asking you to develop this discipline from the greats that came before us, and capture your life daily.

COMPETENCE = CONFIDENCE

Cultivating the miracle of wisdom is the grand builder of confidence. We have a natural drive to want to be more competent in life. Being competent is the grand builder of great confidence. In psychology, they call this the confidence competence loop. The more competent you are, the more confidence you will have. The more confident you are, the more competent you will become. I can write this book with confidence because I studied and became so competent that I believe in the message in this book. The same will happen in your life. If you have the confidence to start, you will build more competence. That, in turn, will build more confidence. Confident people are so competent that they are sure of what they do. (If you want more information on building confidence or would like a free confidence coaching call go to RoyRedd.com and contact Roy and his team.)

The Ying and Yang of Confidence and Competence

THE SUCCESS TRIBE

When Mark Zuckerberg founded Facebook, he understood the importance of being around the right people. If you have seen the movie Social Network about the beginning of Facebook, you would know why. In the movie, Mark and his cofounder, Eduardo Saverin, had frequent arguments about where they needed to move the company. In the movie, Eduardo and Mark have a meeting with Sean Parker, the founder of Napster, an Internet company that allows the downloading of music. Mark looked up to Sean because he had been through the process of building a major Internet company and really made noise in the Internet world. Sean single-handily put stores like Tower Records out of business by being disruptive in the marketplace of music. Eduardo, however, didn't like or trust Sean Parker. He had read things about Sean that made him question Sean's motives. Mark looked up to Sean because he knew that Sean already had the knowledge of what to do, and what not to do, in this type of business. Mark understood the idea of being coached by someone who already had been down the path he wanted to go. Sean told them they needed to move to Palo Alto, California, which is the known place for entrepreneurs to move to.

Palo Alto is to entrepreneurs what Hollywood is to actors. Aspiring actors go to Hollywood to be around and connect with people who can help them on their journey. Mark understood this. He knew he had to get in the game and have the conversations, and clashes, with these people to build his company. Mark knew the importance of developing a successful tribe that understands the business. Since Eduardo was to supply the money, and already wasn't too fond of Sean, he wasn't very happy with this idea. But you can argue that if they had never gone to Palo Alto, they may have never taken off the way they did.

Choosing who you hang around is vital to the person

Your circle is like a bunch of boats in the ocean. If you all live in congruence with a common set of values and beliefs, you all can ride a wave together to the top. The negative side is if you choose the wrong circle, this wave can also take you to the bottom.

you become. Who you hang around determines your philosophies on life. I say this is because if you want to be a wiser person, or make more money, you have to get around wise people. If you are the smartest person in your circle, guess what? It's time for a new circle. I know plenty of people who are very intelligent but end up in jail, or just in a bad place in life, all because they hang around the wrong people.

Human beings are social animals. Being social is the reason that we have succeeded in this world amongst all the outside dangers around us. We aren't the strongest, fastest, or smartest by ourselves. We are strong when we are in groups. As a group, we can do anything.

Back in the Paleolithic era, when we went hunting, we went together. We can't take on a bull or a tiger or a gazelle by ourselves. But when we go together in unison, we can get it done in an amazing way. Since we are so social, we have to be very careful what social circles we belong to. You can't expect to develop a positive, fun life if you hang around negative, boring people. Studies have shown that you can tell everything about a person based on who that person hangs out with.

If a group of woman decides to move in together, something happens over a short period of time. Ask any woman this; she knows. When woman are around each other a lot, their menstrual cycles align to the point they have their cycles at the same time. This is not arbitrary; there is a totally biological reason for this. This is why who you hang around is who you are.

You ever notice how you talk a certain way around certain people and another way around others? I have a friend who cusses a lot, and when I'm around her, I notice that I cuss more. So, I don't hang around this person for long periods of time because after awhile, I'll be cussing just as much as she does. Aristotle said it best: "We can choose what we shall be by choosing now the environment that shall mould us; so we are free in the sense that we mould our own character by our choice of friends." If you want to cultivate wisdom, it's as simple as hanging around wise people.

LEARN FROM THE WISEST MAN EVER

A woman came to the king who ruled over all of Israel looking for justice. When she had awakened from her sleep, she noticed that her baby was dead. After taking a closer look at the baby, she realized the baby was not hers. She came to realize another woman who accidentally killed her own baby had taken her baby and had replaced it with the dead baby during the night. The other woman completely denied these accusations. The baby that was alive was her baby the woman said. The two woman went back and forth arguing about who was the mother of the living baby.

"Bring me my sword," the king said. The king took the living baby and held him up in the air. "I am going to cut this baby in two pieces and you both can take half," he said.

"No, dear king, don't cut the baby. I am not the mother. Give the baby to the other woman," the first woman said.

"Go ahead and cut the baby, dear king, and neither one of us will have a living baby," the second woman said.

"Give the baby to the first woman. She is obviously the mother of this baby," the king said, making his decision.

When the people of Israel heard of the verdict the king had given, they held him in awe because they saw that he had the wisdom from God to administer justice.

When King Solomon was about to take the throne as king, he was extremely nervous. He wanted to be a great king and sincerely do what was right for the people. King Solomon had a great relationship with God. When I say "relationship," I mean he talked to God through prayer on a regular basis. When Solomon was coming to his place on the throne, he had a dream where God appeared. In his dream with God, he expressed his worries about becoming king. He expressed how his father David did such a good job as God's servant, and he wished to do the same. He was nervous because he was so young and didn't know how to be a king. Solomon asked God for wisdom so that he could lead his people in the right direction. He wanted a wise heart so that he could judge 'right from 'wrong. God was happy that Solomon had asked for this, so He answered Solomon's prayers not only with wisdom but also with wealth and honor.

It was pleasing in the sight of the Lord that Solomon had asked this thing. God said to him, "Because you have asked this thing and have not asked for yourself long life, nor have asked riches for yourself, nor have you asked for the life of your enemies, but have asked for yourself discernment to understand justice, behold, I have done according to your words. Behold, I have given you a wise and discerning heart, so that there has been no one like you before you, nor shall one like you arise after you. I have also given you what you have not asked, both riches and honor, so that there will not be any among the kings like you all your days. If you walk in My ways, keeping My statutes and commandments, as your father David walked, then I will prolong your days." (1 Kings 3:10–14, NIV)

King Solomon was the richest, wisest, most powerful man to ever live. This is clear proof of the value of wisdom. I know you may not be religious or believe in the Bible, but I ask you to still learn from the stories. The Bible is such a great book on how life is supposed to be lived. The Bible is just as practical as it is spiritual.

Solomon was so wise that kings and queens from all over the world traveled to seek his counsel. The richest, most powerful people of the world risked everything just to meet Solomon and to learn of his wisdom. If the most powerful people wanted to learn from him, I think I would want to learn from him as well. Solomon wrote the book of Proverbs. Since he is the wisest man to ever live, I take it upon myself to read his wisdom every day. Every day I look at the date, and I read that chapter of Proverbs. I can't tell you the amazing ideas, philosophies, and value this brings me. Every single day I get coaching from the wisest man who ever lived.

I not only read the words from the wisest man to ever live but also use his dream as a catalyst for my prayers. I pray every day when I first wake up and before I go to sleep. I start out with everything I am grateful for. Gratitude is the best emotion that anyone can express. And whether you believe it or not, all blessings come from God Himself. I give thanks for all these blessings no matter how big or how small. After I give thanks, I ask for what I want in my life. "If you ask, you shall receive." When you ask, make sure you ask intelligently. I ask for one thing and one thing only: wisdom. With wisdom, I will have the knowledge to achieve any goal. I don't ask for my problems to go away or to make life any easier. I ask for the wisdom to know how to handle my problems and the knowledge to achieve what I wish to achieve. The story of Solomon gives us the blueprint for what to ask for and 'what is the most important value. So, I ask when you pray to whoever you pray to, ask for wisdom just as Solomon did.

THE ROTTWEILER VERSUS THE CHIHUAHUA

Everybody has a genius inside of them, whether you believe it or not. If you don't believe it, maybe you have not learned to quiet your negative brain. We all have a positive brain and a negative brain. We can go to a place where we get really confident even to the point of arrogance. We can also go to a place of negativity, thinking we can't do anything.

I want to share a secret with you: all the negativity you think about is mostly a lie.

It's all a lie told to you by what psychologists call the lizard brain. The lizard brain is the name they give to the part of the brain called the amygdala. The amygdala is a small walnut-sized part of the brain in charge of nothing but survival instincts. The reason they call it the lizard brain is because this is the only type of brain a lizard has. The amygdala wants only to survive and reproduce, and be angry and fearful. This is the brain of a wild animal. The uncontrolled lizard brain says "I'm hungry, I'm horny, now I'm out of here." If you don't believe you're a genius, all that means is you have not learned to quiet the lizard.

Humans also have the big top part of the brain. This big part of the brain consists of the limbic brain and the neocortex. The limbic brain is the part of the brain dreams and gut feelings come from. The neocortex is the analytical part of the brain. These two parts of the brain are much larger than the lizard brain, but the lizard brain is louder than they are. It's like a little chihuahua versus a big rottweiler. The chihuahua is inferior to the rottweiler in size, so its only chance to make a difference is to bark and make noise. It's up to you to choose which brain to listen to, the calm, big, powerful rottweiler or the loud, small, weak chihuahua.

HOW TO QUIET THE LIZARD

The big part of the brain—let's just call it the genius—is the part of the brain you need to tap into, not the lizard part. The Romans called this part of the brain the daemon, a Greek word for genius. The most effective way to quiet the lizard and tune in to this genius is to meditate. Take some time out of your day, every day, to sit in complete silence, to just sit still. Sitting still in silence gives the genius inside of you a chance to speak. The daemon is smart. It doesn't want to scream and try to out talk the lizard. Instead, it stays quiet until you are silent and ready to listen. There is a difference between a debate and an argument. A debate is sophisticated, where an argument is messy. The lizard wants to argue because it's messy, but the genius wants to debate. It's far more sophisticated. Sitting in quiet meditation is essential to cultivating wisdom. It allows your genius to speak up and tell the negative brain to shut up.

TRUE WISDOM

If you understand the ideas in this section, you will be

amongst the wisest people in the world. Bold statement, isn't it? Please read slowly and with an open mind.

Our lives are dictated by one main thing: our concepts. Our concepts drive all of our actions. Concepts are not just we believe; they are much more powerful than that. Our concepts are we know. 'The statement "I believe" is not as powerful as the statements that articulate what you know without a doubt. Beliefs are the lowest form of knowing something. But when you are sure about something, the statement sounds different. The statement is more along the lines of "I am," "that is," or "they are." Can you feel the difference? There is a huge difference in believing in yourself and knowing yourself.

Concepts are extremely powerful. Concepts are built many different ways: by what you read, what you listen to, what you visualize, and who you decide to spend your time with. The mind is tricky. It will develop concepts based on what you feed it. The habits in this book are far more powerful than getting you to read more, listen to more motivational programs, or change your friends. They are powerful because I am giving you tangible things to do that will manufacture the concepts you need to succeed. Reading this book now is developing and building the important concepts of taking responsibility for your own success. The truly wise person chooses what to read, what to listens to, and who to hang out with, with intention—choosing these things with the intention to build the concepts a person wants in life.

What I want you to get is this:
You must satisfy what the perfect
concepts for you are.
When you do this with your own
self-expression, you will have the
success that you desire.

You have the ability to manufacture and engineer your own concepts with intention by doing this. It's the highest level of enlightenment to know that you are the cause of your own concepts by choosing, with intention, what you feed your mind. Choose your own concepts, not society's concepts, not your parents' concepts, but your own concepts. That's why I define success as the achievement of a future ideal." Dealing with this domain of concepts is tricky because we use concepts to define other concepts.

CHAPTER 6

PROTECT YOUR TEMPLE

The value of your health is vital to your success. If you aren't where you know you should be, healthwise, it's time to act. You can't enjoy anything in life if you're not even healthy enough to be present, energized, and vibrant. Most people talk about the type of health and fitness they want, but they don't actually cultivate this in their life.

I'm relaxing at the station, superexhausted after we've been running 911 calls all day at the Rose Bowl game. It's 9 p.m. I don't want to go to sleep because I know I'll be woken by another call soon. I recline in the chair and watch a movie, as I do on all my 24-hour shifts. Just as the movie is getting good, the phone rings. I pick up the phone to hear my dispatcher's voice on the other end. "Hey, I know you're tired, but I need you en route to a residence in north Pasadena for an unknown medical aid," she says.

"OK, show us en route," I say, trying not to sound irritated.

"They need us en route to a residence in north Pasadena," I tell my partner.

My partner and I play rock-paper-scissors for who gets to drive to the call. I usually win, but this time I lose. I throw on my boots and jacket and sit in the passenger seat waiting on my partner. I pull out the Thomas Guide to get an idea of how to guide my partner and to eyeball what hospitals are near by.

We head to the residence with some random rock 'n' roll song blasting through the speakers as I navigate my partner to the destination. The driver always chooses what we listen to. If I were driving, we would be listening to whatever hip-hop song was on the radio at the time.

We finally get to the residence and check to see if the scene is safe. We walk up to the sixth-floor apartment and realize our dispatcher hadn't given us an apartment number. As we try to contact dispatch, a woman sticks her head out of the window of the sixth floor. "She's up here!" she screams.

This woman is obviously worried, but me and my partner keep our cool as we gather our equipment. We have been through some really tough calls together. Nothing can get us nervous at this point. As we walk up the stairs passing the third floor, a stench hit us in the face. It's a smell—I can't explain—it's a smell both me and my partner are familiar with. "GI bleed," we say at the same time, looking at each other.

We get to the door and are met by the woman who stuck her head out the window. "What's going on today?" I ask.

"My mom been bleeding from her backside for three days, and she passed out earlier today," she replies.

"Why did you call the ambulance today instead of three days ago? Did something get worse or change?" I ask.

"No, besides the fact that she passed out earlier and feels lightheaded, nothing," the lady replies.

As I walk into the room, the smell multiplies by tenfold at least. I look at my partner, and he looks back at me as if to say this is the worst smell in the world. I walk up to the patient and realize there is a huge problem—literally. This lady is the biggest person I have ever seen. I immediately realize that we have no way of getting this lady out the house with just the two of us. I know that time is important, so I send my partner back to the ambulance to call for the fire department to help us with a lift assist. While my partner is calling, I start my assessment.

"Ma'am, my name is Roy. What seems to be the problem today?"

"Hey, baby, I've been bleeding, and I am too weak to get up for the last three days," she replies.

"Can you usually walk?" I ask.

"Yes."

I try to help her stand up, but it obviously 'isn't happening today. My partner comes back asking her weight.

"Ma' am, how much do you weigh?" I ask.

"Last time I checked was a couple weeks ago. I was 650 pounds," she says.

With a straight face I say, "OK, ma'am. Well, we are going to have to come up with a plan to get you to the hospital."

I hear the loud horns of the fire engine pulling up outside, so I walk to the door to meet the firefighters. The fire department hates to be called for things of this sort, especially around this time when they were probably having dinner.

"What's going on?" a fireman asks.

I tell him the situation, and he understands why we called for help. He walks in to eyeball the patient and then picks up his radio to call for additional help. This 600-pound lady is on the sixth floor—and she is bleeding to death. As we all stand around giving our input on how to get her out, I finally come up with an idea.

"Let's just put her on a piece of tarp and drag her down the stairs. That's the only way we can do it," I say, shrugging my shoulders.

The fire captain agrees. And that's what we do. It takes two 'EMTs, four police officers, and eleven fireman to get this lady down to the ambulance.

After we load her in the back of the ambulance and head to the hospital, I start thinking: "How can anyone get to this point? How can someone literally eat themselves to being 600 pounds and not ever do anything about it? This lady did not care about her health at all it seemed."

Finally, after these thoughts bug me long enough, I say to her in a concerned voice, "Ma'am, I don't mean to be rude, but how could you let yourself get like this? You deserve to be in better health for your kids and family, and most importantly for yourself. This isn't the way to live, ma'am."

She begins to cry. "I know, I know," she whimpers.

GUARD THE TEMPLE

Sickness is detrimental to the value of health. Sickness looks for its chance to come in and disrupt everything that it can. Viruses and bacteria look for any opening they can to attack your well-being. They are lurking and waiting. Waiting for you to not get enough sleep, not drink enough water, or get stressed out so they can attack when you're most vulnerable. When our body is at its maximum health, it is very rare for us to get sick. Our white blood cells are ready to attack any virus or bacterium as soon as it surfaces. This is why viruses hide like a coward, waiting for their opportunity, waiting for the white blood cells to decrease in power. If your body is a temple, your white blood cells are the guards of this temple. Viruses are the looters watching and waiting for the guards to leave or be weakened so that they can come into the temple and steal its treasures. Don't let this happen to you. Keep your guards up and keep sickness at a distance.

– The First Guard: Diet

Your diet is the first and most important guard that watches over the temple. Being aware of what you put in your body is vital to staying healthy. Most people think of their diet as something that determines what their body looks like, which is true. But your diet also contributes to how you feel, how much energy you have, and keeping diseases away.

Your body is made for certain foods to be taken in. In my opinion all diets are dumb but for sake of argument I would argue that the proper diet for our bodies is a Paleo diet take or give different circumstances. The Paleo diet consists of lean meats, vegetables, fruit, and nuts. These foods are the foundation of what built our brains and keep us healthy and energized to take on the day. But this is not a diet book. Using this diet isn't what matters. What matters is that you generally eat healthy. Doesn't matter what diet you choose. Like I said, in my opinion all diets are dumb, I happen to believe in knowing our own bodies, and we are all different. The absolute best way to find out what works for you is by comparing and contrasting different foods. We all know that McDonald's makes us feel like crap, and if we eat too much of it, we will, without a doubt, end up overweight and sick. I'm not saying you can't eat bad foods in moderation, but for the most part, your food intake should be healthy and clean.

– Six Liters a Day

Anyone who is active should be drinking at least six liters of water a day. Our bodies are made up of 70 percent water. Water keeps us healthy, energetic, and hydrated for high performance. The proper amount of water allows nutrients to be transported through your body properly. It also allows for healthy growth of your hair, nails, and skin. Water keeps your immune system working at a high level so that your white blood cells work properly. The proper intake of water allows the cells in your body to multiply at the rate in which they are suppose to. Having proper mitosis (cell division) is vital for staying healthy, sustaining energy, and remaining hydrated. I know that sounds like common sense, but is this common sense actual common practice in your life? You might want to take a hard headed look at your actions and results.

– Energy

In 2004, a company in Wabash, Indiana, realized the importance of energy and how everyone desired to have more. The company came up with a small drink that claimed to give people quick and sustaining energy. The product was an instant success. People bought this shot of energy to make it through their day without the lag that bad eating contributes to. Today, Living Essentials, LLC, the maker of

5-Hour Energy drink, is a billion-dollar company. How did a small company that sells energy shots catapult to a billion dollars in sales? Simply because energy is a priceless force that everyone wants.

We all have that friend who is always superhigh in energy, and we wonder why that person is so successful. Energy is the secret to becoming as productive as you wish to be. The reason that the makers of drinks such as 5-Hour Energy, Red Bull, Rockstar, and Monster Energy do so well is people's lack of natural energy. Most people eat bad, don't drink enough water, or don't get a good night's sleep, as they should. The result of this is the masses of people walking around drained in a zombie-like trance. Since almost everyone wants a quick fix instead of getting down to the actual problem, energy drinks have become a hot commodity. Energy drinks are a shortcut to a quick burst of energy now. And when you can get a quick burst of energy every day with a quick drink, why should anyone eat better, drink more water, or sleep more? The problem with that philosophy is that the energy never sustains itself. With all the peak performance energy drinks give you, you will meet a valley on the other side. You will always come back down and get addicted to drinking these drinks just to have enough energy to get by.

I work with a doctor who drinks five to ten Monster Energy beverages every time he works. The guy at work always has high energy to the point he seems tweaked out. In the long run, he loses energy and ends up dead tired, not to mention whatever heart problems or kidney problems the drinks might cause. The true key to high energy is a good diet, drinking plenty of water, and getting at least seven hours of sleep. If you do these things, with some exercise daily, you will have a heightened amount of energy and will rarely get sick.

Your body uses food as its energy source, just as a car uses gas. So, think of your body as a Porsche 911 that needs the best gas possible to run at a high level. Would you put 87 regular gas in your Porsche? Of course not. You are going to use the highest octane gas you can possibly use so that your car runs the best it can. Your body runs the same way. You can't put bad fuel in your body and then expect to have high energy. That's like planting grape seeds and expecting oranges to grow—it's not going to happen. When it comes to energy, you get what you put in—literally. When you start to eat healthy and you feel the energy levels it creates, you'll be surprised at what you can get done. You will have the energy to take on any task life throws at you, with force.

You know how if you go to a long time without eating, you tend to lose your patience and become a little more annoyed at things that usually wouldn't annoy you? That's because the energy you receive from food balances your mood. You can drink an energy drink to stay awake, but it won't keep your mood regulated so that you have a good day. Food also energizes your brain so that you can think critically as needed. Studies have shown that students who have a big test score much better if they eat breakfast. Our brains require a high amount of glucose (sugar) to think at a high level. When I teach my Basic Life Support for health care providers class, I try to keep chips and candy available for students before the test. The salt and the sugar allow for better brain functioning during the exam. I've noticed a big difference when I don't serve the snacks. People miss questions they generally know the answers to when they don't eat before the test because they lack the focus that food helps create. So, before you stuff your face with food, consider how you are going to feel after eating the food and if it is going to give you the energy to be productive and to think sharp. Don't eat just anything. Be aware of the gas you are putting in your beautiful Porsche 911.

3 Ways to Cultivate Your Health Value
1. Make sure you are healthy enough to live.
2. Live with energy and vibrancy.
3. Take your health to another level to where you're proud of your fitness and how you look.

— Everybody Wants to Look Good
The last reason, and often times what drives many people to cultivate the value of health, is to look good. Most of us want a nice body. The people who say they don't care

about having a nice body are the people who use that as an excuse not to strive for the body they really want. Looks are not everything, 'not even a value in my eyes, but I'm saying it's a strong reason to get in shape. Imagine having the body you want. What would that do for your confidence? I suggest you set a physical goal and strive to attain it. I had a goal to get my body fat down to 6 percent, and I was able to achieve that with good habits. My confidence was at an all-time high. I was quick to take my shirt off if the situation called for it, eager to show off my abs and cuts. It's not about being superhubris and showing off all the time. It's about feeling good about yourself and proud that you have achieved your goal.

Visit www.royredd.com and contact Roy to get a free framework to help you reach your fitness goals.

The best way to increase your confidence is to achieve something you told yourself that you would do. Telling yourself you are going to get fit and never doing it is detrimental to your confidence. Deciding to be physically fit is at the core of cultivating the value of health. For any decision you make, to keep that promise to yourself, you need strong reasons why you want to accomplish it. Looking good is a strong reason that moti-

Having the body you want is not what builds your confidence. What builds your confidence is knowing you set out to achieve a goal and you achieved it.

vates people to be physically fit. If you won't cultivate your health for the energy, or for the brainpower, do it simply because you want to look good with your shirt off. Do it simply because you want to look good for your wife. Do is simply because of the way it will make you feel inside.

HUNTING FOR FOOD

Today, we no longer need to hunt, but we can still get the same high our ancestors got from hunting, just by working out, by running, by lifting weights, or by doing yoga. Running actually hurts. Lifting weights actually hurts. Doing yoga actually hurts. So, why does it feel so good? It's a Catch 22. That good feeling is called the runners high. But there are kinds of highs from hunting and exercising.

The group gathers around the outside of the cave, pumped up and hungry. The fastest, strongest, and most alpha males prepare to perform the most important task for the group. It's time to go hunting. The group sets out to find food for the tribe, ready for the hard, long, exhausting work it takes to hunt gazelle in the wild. Gazelles are much faster than humans are—it's no contest. When the gazelles get wind of the group, they are sure to take off running, and even the fastest person in the tribe has no chance of running them down. That's OK. Humans are endurance animals. We can hunt for hours at a time and even days if needed.

The hunters spot the herd of gazelle and sneak up on it. They look to the most intelligent person in the group for ideas on how to do this. As they try to sneak up, one of the gazelles spots them and runs. When one gazelle runs, all of the gazelles run. One of the gazelles is sick, so the group tracks it down and kills it as the other gazelles run away, increasing the distance between them. The hunters can't feed the whole tribe with one gazelle, so they keep tracking the herd as it runs. The hunters run after the gazelle knowing they don't have the speed to catch them. It's OK, though. They know the gazelle can run fast for only short spurts, but the hunters can keep a good pace for hours at a time. They keep on the chase making the gap between them and their soon-to-be dinner smaller and smaller.

As hunters close in, the gazelle frantically scatter again, running as fast as they can to get away from sure death. The 'hunters aren't worried about it. They are in this for the long haul. As they get their second wind, they aren't hurting or tired at all. They continue to narrow the gap again and again and again until eventually they catch the gazelle. By now, the gazelle are too tired to outrun the hunters.

They kill the gazelle, tie them up, and get ready for the long walk home. On the way home with the prize in hand, they share their thoughts about today's hunt with a smile on their faces. They feel a surge of confidence because they went out and did what they needed to do to feed their families. They get back to the village. Bodies are tired. Bones are achy. Muscles are sore. They are in pain.

"Same time tomorrow," the leader says.

The other hunters look at him, feeling good about today's hunt. "Yes, same time tomorrow," they reply.

The question is, why? Why, when they are in pain from the hunt, are they so willing to go again. Of course, they have to eat, but that isn't the only factor at play here. They don't need to go tomorrow. They have enough food to last a week. Why were they able to track the gazelle for hours at a time? Why did it feel so good to put stress on their bodies physically?

You do realize running miles at a time actually hurts your body? It's physically draining. It hurts your muscles. It uses up all your nutrients. Although it does all these things, it still feels amazing when you are done. Does it feel amazing because we know mentally it's improving our stamina, strength, and looks? No, not at all. When we lift weights trying to get stronger and more toned, it actually puts tremendous strain on our bodies. But when we are done working out, it feels great. Is that because we know we are improving? Maybe, partially, but it's not why we feel amazing when we are done. When we are in yoga class stretching, twisting, and holding extremely hard positions, that actually puts strain on the body. It's good for the body in the long run, but to improve, we first must go through the pain. But why, when we are done going through these workouts that actually beat up the body, do we feel like we can take over the world?

THE BODY'S CHEMISTRY

– *Endorphins*

The answer to these questions is endorphins. Endorphins are a special chemical released by the body to mask pain. Generally, endorphins are like a narcotic, but 'they are produced from your body and 'not addictive like morphine is, for example. Endorphins are a genius way that our body rewards us and keeps us going for doing things that are good for our well-being. When we work out, we release these endorphins to mask the pain that we inflict on our bodies. It feels good to run for miles for improvement. It feels good to lift heavy weights for improvement. It feels good to do yoga and stretch ourselves for improvement. The human body realizes how good it is for us to improve physically, so it sets a system to reward us for this. The reward for this improvement is the good feeling you get when you work out, the good feeling of endorphins.

When the hunters set out to hunt, the reason they were able to track the gazelle for hours was the endorphins. The endorphins masked the pain of running for hours until they were able to get the job done. If working out just hurt, and we didn't get the feeling of endorphins, would people still work out? I don't know the answer to that question, but I wouldn't think so. Your body wants to improve; it wants to get stronger, faster, and healthier. The proof is in the reward it gives you. The reward of the great feeling you get when you actually cultivate your value of fitness.

- *LOL*

Endorphins are also released when you laugh. Laughing is good for you, and your body wants you to do it more. So, the way it rewards you is also with endorphins. When you laugh, you actually shake and move your internal organs. You shake your organs to the point that it can hurt. This is why your body chooses endorphins for this purpose as well. It masks physical pain. We've all had that time when we laughed with friends for so long that the endorphins actually ran out. That's why when you were laughing so hard and so long, you looked at your friend, and said, "Stop. Stop. It hurts." It hurts because you used all your endorphins that your body had for laughing at the time. Some things that hurt us actually make us better. Your body helps you out by masking that pain with endorphins.

- *Cortisol*

Exercise does amazing things not only for your body but also for your brain. Exercise releases certain chemicals that help your brain deal with stress. The feelings of stress, anxiety, and nervousness come from cortisol, a chemical in your body. Cortisol raises pulse rate, blood pressure, and respiratory rate. Cortisol's job is to get us ready for a fight or flight reaction in response to certain stimuli. It gets us ready to react to whatever is attacking us. We tend to release this chemical even when we don't have anything attacking, based on the story we tell ourselves about the stimulus. There is no way of getting rid of stress in your life. The only thing you can do is deal with it the best way you can. Stress is actually good for us to a point. Stress with proper recovery is the key to all improvement. So, if you're progressing in life, you're going to have stress. To deal with the stresses of life, you must exercise daily.

– Brain-Derived Neurotrophic Factor

When you exercise a special protein called brain-derived neurotrophic factor (BDNF) is released. This protein does a bunch of wonderful things for your body. The one thing we care about is its ability to help us deal with stress. This protein protects the neurons in your brain that control your mood. So, when cortisol is released, and if you exercise, this protein protects your mood from the stress. It also protects your hippocampus from being affected by the stress. The hippocampus is the part of the brain that allows us to remember things and learn things. So, BDNF not only help us with stress but also keeps us from remembering that stress for the future. This is important because sometimes we can have a bad experience and let that experience change our outlook toward whatever caused the bad experience. For example: If you were mugged by an African American male, does that mean all African American males are muggers? Of course not. But if you don't have a proper amount of BDNF in your body and you go through that experience, you will have a strong bias toward African American males. You may know intellectually that not all African American males 'are muggers. But when you see one, your body will release cortisol in reaction to its past memories unless you have a healthy amount of BDNF that keeps that bias from engraving on your hippocampus. Exercise improves your body physically and mentally. Exercise is a great way and, I would argue, the best way to regulate your well-being.

HUNTERS TURNED FARMERS

This is what we were made for and were built for—to hunt, to get together as one and use our minds and bodies to catch food. It takes a lot of brainpower, physical strength, and teamwork to catch supper. Our ancestors were very intelligent, fit, and social because of this. It takes a lot of brainpower to think and do physical things at the same time. The problem came when we became too smart for our own good, when we decided to raise our food instead of hunt for it. Farming doesn't take as much brainpower, physicality, or teamwork as hunting does.

I would argue that farming has made us weaker. It has

given us more food in the long run, but at what cost? The food isn't always good for us. We don't hunt, which allowed us to get a workout. And we lack the teamwork skills we once had. Now, I'm not saying to get your friends together and go take on a bear. I am saying if we can't hunt, we must do the things closest to hunting that we can. Eat the lean foods that we had when we hunted. Exercise because that's the closest thing we have to the physicality of hunting. And become part of a strong social power circle. If we cultivate these things, we will be healthier and better off, and we will be strong and smart like our ancestors were.

STARTING IS THE HARD PART

When it comes to anything, but especially working out, starting is the hardest part. If you set a goal to do 100 push-ups a day, the hardest push-up isn't the last one. The hardest push-up is the first one. Working out and cultivating the value of health isn't hard at all. Running the miles or lifting the weights or doing the yoga stretches are not the hard part at all. It's not hard because of the endorphins in your body. But what is hard is to be proactive enough to start.

Every day when I finish a 12-hour shift at work, I go to the gym. Every day 'on my way home I feel tired and don't want to work out. I make up excuses for why I shouldn't go that day. (We will talk about why the brain does this later. It's hard every single day to just get in the gym and start. The thing is, I know that once I start, I'll be more than

OK. Once I get the first couple sets in, I know that I'll feel amazing from my endorphin high, and I will power through the workout with force. It's like someone is holding a bottle of "feel good" for you, but the only way to get it is to start.

Successful people and unsuccessful people have one thing in common: neither wants to do what it takes to succeed. The difference is successful people just do it anyway. I have found that when you are competent, and know the forces at work in the battle of personal development, you tend to force yourself because you know how it all works. Now that you know why you feel good after a workout, hopefully, you will work out. Now that you know the hardest part about getting it done, you will get it done. Lots of trainers make their money teaching how to become fit, but none of them teach why. The how doesn't matter if you don't know the why. When you know how to do something, you can come up with excuses to not do it. But when you know the why, you implement the how and achieve maximum results. So now that you know why working out is so important, get off your butt, make a plan, and start today. Now that you know there is a bottle of "feel good" waiting for you, go get it.

CHAPTER 7

SPREAD THE LOVE DRUG

Love is the most powerful force on earth. It wasn't the big nails that held Jesus on the cross—it was love. The love he had for all people, even those persecuting him. What is love? God is Love.

Some time in January of 1987, she starts to have nausea and vomiting and doesn't feel good at all.' Along with the vomiting, she may be a little late in her monthly cycle at the time. She makes a doctor's appointment to see what's going on. During her appointment, the doctor finds the reason for the symptoms—she is pregnant. She makes more doctors' appointments and plans to accommodate the soon to be newest member of the family.

Doctors' appointments, crazy emotions, and a craving for certain foods add to her life. Eighteen to twenty weeks in, she has an ultrasound and finds out she's having a baby boy. She's already raising two kids, mostly on her own: a young woman that she took in and a young man that she birthed five years before.

Weeks go by and everything is on course, going as planned. She's at dinner for her birthday on August 5th, eating multiple plates of food to feed her and the other soul she's carrying. Halfway through the dinner something out of the ordinary happens: her water breaks.

"This can't be happening. The baby's not due until October," she says.

Family members rush her to the hospital to find out what's going on. When they get there, doctors tell her she is in labor, and she's going to have this baby tonight. Wondering about the health of the baby, considering the two-month prematurity, everybody is on edge. She can't believe this is happening, especially since her father told her she was going to have the baby early and on her birthday. They've had an ongoing bet that if she did have the baby on her birthday, she had to name the baby after him. A couple hours goes by as the tension builds in the waiting room.

Finally, after hours of labor, she delivers a premature, but healthy, four-pound baby boy.

She's extremely happy and feels a tremendous surge of love moving through her body as she holds and looks at the baby.

"Have you picked out a name yet?" the doctor asks.

"His name is Roy."

Anybody who knows me knows that I'm a big mama's boy. What they don't know about me is that I was born on my mother's birthday. The love and bond between me and my mother is second to none. It's unconditional love that absolutely nothing can break. The mothers and fathers reading this understand exactly what I'm talking about. The love you have for your kids is unbelievable to you. No matter how your kids come out, you, as a parent, don't judge them; you just love them with all your heart. True love is the bond between mother and son, father and daughter, mother and daughter, father and son. But what causes this strong love and bond? If we could understand why this love is so strong and this bond is so strong, maybe we could cultivate love with others as well. Some might say that the love and bond between parent and child is just natural, which is correct but not the only factor. Something else is at play here.

Some kind of distinct force is the reason for this love and bond that can't be broken, and this force can be used to love others. This force can be used to love your spouse, your family, and your friends. This force is responsible for destroying hate. This force can even cure diseases and addictions.

THE SECRET FORCE OF LOVE

Love is a force that can literally move mountains. Health mountains, hatred mountains, addictive mountains, depressive mountains. But what is actually at play here? How come this force can do all these things? Remember when I told you that our bodies release chemicals to reward us for behavior that's beneficial to us? Well, love does the same thing. The feeling you get when you're in love is caused by a chemical called oxytocin. Oxytocin is the most powerful of all of the chemicals your body releases, in my opinion. This chemical does some really important things that help our well-being in a major way.

What if you had a secret drug that could cure any illness? Well, one way oxytocin helps our well-being is by boosting our immunity. Oxytocin (the feeling of love) actually makes you healthier. This is the reason why married people live longer than single people do. This is why you always see those 90-year-old couples still kicking like they never lost a step. This is also why when we don't feel loved, we get depressed and stressed, and we literally get sick.

Alcoholics Anonymous has been curing people of addictions for a long time now. They have come up with a proven system that helps cure people of their addiction to alcohol. There are 12 steps in the whole process, but the first and last steps are the most important. A large percentage of the people addicted to alcohol will drink again if they don't complete these 2 steps out of the 12. The first step is to have the awareness that you actually have a drinking problem. If you do not know something is broken, you cannot fix it. The second step, which is also the last step in the process, is to help someone get over their addiction after you have gotten over yours. The reason for this is that giving your time to help someone actually releases oxytocin. The person you help gets oxytocin, so it helps stop their addiction, and you get some oxytocin as well, so it stops your addiction.

Oxytocin is contagious. When you give someone love, most people want to reciprocate and give love back. This is why you can't stop hate with hate; you can only stop hate with love. When this person receives that love (oxytocin), she will naturally want to reciprocate and show love back. The question is how do you release oxytocin? Love is not a feeling. Love is not an action or a decision. One of these alone isn't love. You need all three. Love is a decision to act that makes you and others feel loved. Let's look at some actions that cause love.

– *Acts of Generosity*

You know that feeling you get when you help someone even though you didn't have to? That amazing feeling you get when you just help for no reason. Generosity is helping someone and expecting absolutely nothing in return.

I'm driving along and see a women whose car had broken down. I pull my car over behind hers and get out to help.

I tell the lady, "When the light changes, steer it across the street, and Ill push for you."

The light turns green, and I push her car across the street to a safe area. When we are done, she gets out the car and is very thankful for my help. She 'can't seem to believe that I have taken my time to stop and help her. She tries to give me some money for helping her. Of course, I 'don't take it.

"Is there anything I can do for you?" she asks.

I didn't stop to help her because I wanted anything in return. I was just helping a fellow human being when she needed it. I run back to my car and then across the street to a convenience store.

As I was walk into the store, a guy in front of the store stops me. "Hey, man, that was really cool what you did back there," he says.

I smile and go along with my day.

The amazing thing about oxytocin is that it's contagious. One way to release oxytocin is through acts of generosity. It can't be any regular act either. It has to be something that takes time and energy. Although I give money to lofty causes, giving money does not release oxytocin. Giving money isn't valuable to love because it doesn't require time or energy. We can always make more money, but we can't get back time or energy.

If I told you I gave $500 to the children's hospital, what would you think? You might say good for you and shrug your shoulders. But if I told you I went to the children's hospital and spent a whole day volunteering, what would you think? You would say, "Awesome, I need to volunteer more." That is more valuable to a person because it takes my time and energy. This is why if you have kids, you must spend time and energy with them rather than just give them money or gifts.

What's more valuable to kids, buying them a game or going to their game? That's a no-brainer. The reason is oxytocin, the time and energy. When I took a little bit of my time and energy to help that lady, it gave me a dose of oxytocin. I felt good about helping her. At the same moment I got a dose of oxytocin, and I felt good, the lady also got a surge of oxytocin, and she felt good. She didn't just feel good because her car was out of the street. She felt good that a fellow human being took his time and energy to help her.

Another amazing thing about oxytocin is that witnessing acts of generosity releases it as well. When I was walking into the store, and the guy gave me props for what I did, his veins had oxytocin flowing in them as well. I'm pretty sure he did something generous for someone later that day. Oxytocin (love) is contagious.

I stopped to help that lady because I've seen it done

many times before. When I was a kid, my father would always stop to help people if they needed it. I can recall at least a dozen or so times my dad would get out and help push somebody's car out of the road. When I got older, after seeing my dad do it my whole life, I naturally did it as well. If someone needs help, and I'm not pressed for time, I stop to help them every time. I give credit for this habit to my father. Your kids don't do what you say. They only do what they see you do, so I'm grateful to have an amazing father that set a good example. The biological reason behind me following in his footsteps is oxytocin, of course. Remember, oxytocin is released when we see someone do acts of generosity. So, every time I saw my dad do these acts of kindness, I had the powerful force of oxytocin surging through my young veins, teaching me as well to help others. We are social creatures that need help and need to help others. This is why God has given us this force of oxytocin—to reward us and give us incentive to be kind and generous. Generosity is love. Generosity is Godlike.

- *Physical Touch*

Another way to release oxytocin is through physical touch. When you hug, hold, or kiss someone, oxytocin is produced. This is why cuddling feels so good—your body is producing high levels of the love chemical. Every day you should hug your kids. Kiss them, as well as your spouse. Show love with physical acts that make them feel loved. When your kids see mom and dad show affection physically, it releases oxytocin in them as well. A warning comes through.

When people lack love in their life, they go looking for it. This can cause some people to look for physicality in the wrong areas. We've all heard about the woman who slept with the wrong person, looking for the love her parents never gave her. Don't mistake the physical feeling you get for actual love. Remember, love is the decision to act that makes you and others feel good. So, make sure you make the right decisions about who you actually love.

Having sex with someone releases a tremendous amount of oxytocin, so you have to be very careful who you lay with. I don't believe in sleeping with someone just for the sex because the release of oxytocin will start to form a false bond. This is why you don't make decisions about your relationship during or right after sex. You're so full of oxytocin you may think with your emotions, not your head.

So use physical touch as a tool to show your love to those who you decide deserve it. Hug, kiss, and hold your spouse and children. Show your loved ones the love they deserve.

– *Love and Trust*

Some say that love and trust are one and the same. I read once that "love is giving someone the power to destroy you but trusting them not to." A lot of people say they don't trust someone based on that person's past actions. Or they do trust someone based on actions. But trust isn't a decision. You don't decide to trust someone. Trust is actually a feeling. We all have family members who did something untrustworthy, but we still trust them. Or we may know someone who has done many trustworthy things for us, but we still don't trust them. Trust comes from a bond that we accumulate with other people through time and love. This is why it takes years until you ask someone to marry you. Yes, it's also to learn more about the person, but it's also until you trust that person to the point the love is unconditional.

This bond is built through the release of oxytocin over time. Think of it as an oxytocin meter. There is a certain buildup of oxytocin and a certain point that you must hit before you trust someone. So, you give a little oxytocin here and a little oxytocin there until you hit that line. Everyone's meter is different. We all know someone who falls in love overnight, or someone who never wants to trust or commit. When a mother gives birth, she releases an enormous amount of oxytocin during the birth. This is also one of the reasons birth is possible to make it through—there is a reward at the end. A reward of the most love you have ever felt. Think about it. Giving birth is the second most painful thing behind being burnt alive. Why would someone want to go through something like that? The reason is the blessing that the pain comes with and the powerful force of oxytocin (love) with it. Giving birth releases so much oxytocin it hits a woman's trust line in one oxytocin surge.

Trust takes time and energy to earn. No one really knows how long it takes. I guess it's different for everyone.

Oxytocin is also the reason why we shake hands to make a deal. If you make an important deal with someone, and 'that person doesn't shake your hand, you tend not to trust him. You can have all the contracts signed, and everything can look great, but if you don't seal it with a handshake, it doesn't feel right. Shaking hands releases a small amount of oxytocin that allows you to trust the person enough to make the deal. I take shaking hands seriously. When I meet someone, I want them to remember me, as well as like me. I put on a big cheesy smile, look them in the eye, introduce myself, and shake their hand. When I shake their hand, it's a sign of respect, of course, but it also releases oxytocin so that they trust me initially. Nobody trusts the guy who walks into a room and doesn't introduce himself. 'This is considered disrespectful' because it doesn't release oxytocin.

– *Love Your Spouse*

We all know how terrible life can be if we aren't in congruence with our spouse. We also know how great life can be when we are on the same page and everything is clicking. From the man's perspective, when things are going good with his wife, life is great. He goes to work and takes on the day with confidence and ambition, knowing he has support at home. When things aren't going right at home, it obviously shows up in a man's work. He doesn't attack the day the way he does when everything is good. I can't speak from a woman's perspective, but it's obviously better when loved ones are loving to one another.

So, how can you keep the love fresh, vibrant, and full of oxytocin? It's simple. I think every couple should read The Five Love Languages by Gary D. Chapman. In this book, Gary argues that everyone has, what he calls, a "love language." A love language is a way to show your love to your spouse. Each individual values a certain love language more than the others. Gary argues that if you find out your spouse's love language, all you have to do is act in congruence with that language regularly. For example if your spouses love language is physical touch you must hug, kiss, and cuddle with them on a regular.

Gary Chapman's 5 Languages of Love
1. Words of affirmation
2. Physical touch
3. Quality time
4. Random gifts
5. Acts of service

I would argue that physical touch, quality time, and acts of service are everyone's love language. I say this because these three love languages release oxytocin, which gives us the feeling and bond of love. That leaves words of affirmation and random gifts. If your spouse's love language is one of these, I would incorporate them into the others. Every day cultivate the language of physical touch. Hug your spouse before you leave. Kiss her when you get back home. Imagine how much better her day would be if you filled them up with oxytocin. Touch her, kiss her, hold her every day no matter what.

Quality time is a hard language to cultivate simply because we all are busy for the most part. You and your spouse work long hours. The best way to cultivate this language, I have found, is simply by allocating some time every week for spending time together. One day a week have a date night, or do whatever you can to spend time with each other—just you two. Also, make sure you continually perform acts of service for your mate. Open her door, cook his meal, do the things that brought you together consistently. Do whatever it took to get the job so that you can keep the job.

– *Gold*

Love is a powerful positive force that can cure any negative force. I think, as a whole, we should spread love to everyone. The Bible says, "Love your neighbor as yourself." This means you should love everyone and show love to everyone. In today's world, there is still talk of racism, sexism, and homophobia. People share their opinions in these areas with anger and hatred. We should all be proud of where we come from, as well our opinions. Debate and dialogue are part of who we are as human beings. But we should never forget that we are all in this life thing together. One of my favorite ideas ever is by Thich Nhat Hanh, the Zen Buddhist monk. He said, "We are here to awaken from our illusion of separateness." This quote says it all. We are all here for the purpose of helping each other. This is why we have done so well as a species—we stick together.

I believe that God has given us all gifts for helping others. Our gifts aren't for us. They are for the world. A good friend of mine, Jeffrey Osborne, started a movement called GOLD—Giving Out Love Daily. You can check him out at www.Jefftosborne.com in the G.O.L.D. section. The whole idea of the movement is to spread love through acts of generosity. Once you perform an act of generosity for someone, you take the GOLD band off your wrist and give it away. When you give it away, you ask the other person to spread the love. This movement is so powerful because it packages the strongest force known to humans and helps spread it. It spreads oxytocin along with all its perks to the whole community. We should all give out love daily and release the force of oxytocin to everyone near and far.

– Elos, Philia, and Charis

The Greeks believed that there were three levels of love people needed to obtain: elos, philia, and charis.

The first level is to have tremendous love for yourself. The Greeks called this type of love elos. Elos is to have unconditional love for yourself because without love for yourself, you will never be able to love others. You can't love anyone or anything more than you can love yourself. You can't love your spouse more than you love yourself. You can't love your kids more than you love yourself. And you can't love your family more than you love yourself. To think you can love someone or something more than yourself is naive. If you can't accept the way you are, how can you ever accept the way someone else is? If you can't accept the way you look, how can you teach your kids to accept the way they look? The only way to reflect love outward is to first have it inward. You can't give out something that you don't already have.

The second level of love, according to the Greeks, is called philia. At the philia level of love, you are able to express love to others. Remember, you can't give what you don't have, so if you can't achieve elos, how will you ever achieve philia? When we love ourselves and accept ourselves, our natural tendency is to spread the love to others. Whenever you have self-love and you feel blessed in any way, the natural thing to do is to pay it forward in any way you can. Remember oxytocin is contagious. Self-love makes us big-hearted and generous in everything we do. When we reach out to be generous and spread the love that we feel for ourselves, 'we have reached the philia level of love.

The last, and most difficult level of love to reach, the Greeks called charis. The charis level of love refers to having love for everyone. The charis level of love says" you have love for all of humankind." This is the hardest level of love to reach. It requires a lot of self-development. When I think of this level of love, it reminds me of having the best possible character. The character to love everyone—no matter where they are from, what they look like, or what they have.

When they selected the new pope, I watched the decision on TV like everyone else. They showed a video of Pope Francis going to an HIV clinic to pray for the people there. One of the patients at the clinic was really sick, and the pope prayed over him. He washed the man's feet, prayed for him, then kissed his feet as a blessing. If that's not charis, then I don't know what is! That's the love to generally care and spend your time loving others. This is the level of love Jesus Christ had. This is the love that held Him on the cross for all of our sins. This is the love I imagine God has, plus some. This is the type of love had Him send His one and only son to earth for the sake of freeing humankind. This is the type of love that at our very best we can only hope to achieve.

– Loving Yourself

I want to return to the idea of loving yourself. Loving yourself is important to cultivate in order to have the capacity to love others. I believe the most important love you can have is self-love. You can always tell the level of love someone has for themselves by how they loves others. But what prevents people from loving themselves? I propose the following five steps to develop self-love.

– *Step 1: accept yourself exactly how you are.*

You must accept the person you are, mentally, physically, and spiritually. You are one of a kind, literally. God made you in His image, and you are perfect in your own way. Don't let the stigma of how people are suppose to be or look affect how you feel about yourself. I always tell people that I'm gorgeous, not to be hubris, but because I know I am. I know that God made me in His image, and I accept how He made me. People care about how others see them more than how God sees them. That's absolutely, positively "blasfamous" (in my best Steven A. Smith impression.) What people think about you doesn't say anything about you; it says everything about them. If someone thinks you're ugly, maybe they just feel like they are ugly and can only make themselves feel better by calling you ugly. Another thing people do is use the wrong wording for how they describe someone. Someone can say you're not attractive, but that's not because you aren't attractive. That is just that person's opinion. Accept yourself. Who cares what others say? They do not have permission to speak into your life.

– *Step 2: accept full responsibility for your life.*

Accept all the things that happen to you and all the consequences of your actions. When you become self-reliant, you refuse to criticize and blame others. In psychology, this is called having a causal mindset. A causal mindset means you are the cause of everything that happens to you in your life. People want to make outside excuses on why things happen to them when it was their doing all along. People blame outside forces because it's hard to put the blame on yourself. It's easier to soothe yourself with the excuses, or what unsuccessful people call reasons, to protect your pride. The problem with making excuses is you never become disgusted enough to fix the problem. You never get down to the roots of problems because you think outside forces caused it instead of yourself. Having a causal mindset is essential to having high self-esteem, high self-love, and high effectiveness. Get some causal agency in your mind, and strive to take responsibility.

— *Step 3: set goals that stretch you.*

Setting goals that stretch you gives you something to strive for, which boosts your confidence. (Go to www.royredd.com to get a free ebook Finish: 7 secrets to achieve your goals.) Only a person with self-confidence has the confidence to set goals. Writing down and setting goals requires you to do something about it. If you write down a goal and don't achieve it, it can have a bad effect on your pride. This is why people are afraid to write their goals. If they don't achieve their goals, their pride gets hurt. Only a prideful, confident person can write down his goals with the resolve to achieve them. When you have achieved a goal, think of what that did for your confidence. Setting goals is a way to demonstrate that you take responsibility for your life. It is the secret to taking total control of your destiny.

– *Step 4: take care of yourself physically.*

We have talked about the feeling you get when you have pride in your health and the way you look. The more you eat better, work out, and control your health, the better you feel about yourself. The better you feel about yourself, the more self-love you have. The best part is when you have this self-love for yourself, you start to spread it to others. The better you feel about yourself, the better you feel about others.

– *Step 5: affirm yourself.*

The fastest way to feel more love for yourself is through self-affirmation. To affirm to yourself how great you are, how good you look, and how smart you are. You have to affirm how you think about yourself until it sets deep into your subconscious. Talk to yourself. Tell yourself how good you are. This may sound weird, but we talk to ourselves all the time. The next time talk to yourself to affirm the truth of your greatness. I tell myself all the time, "Good job, Roy, You did that!" Give yourself permission to congratulate yourself. God created this whole universe with words, so you do the same with your words. Tell yourself how good you look today. It's not a lie; it's absolutely true.

Affirming yourself with good words comes with a warning though. You can't just affirm yourself without also acting in congruence with those affirmations. Yes, affirm how beautiful you are because, yes, you are beautiful. But don't affirm how healthy you are if you're not working out and eating right.

Self-affirming without acting is like watering soil with no seed in it. Affirm your amazingness and act on it daily.

"Affirmations without discipline is the beginning of an illusion." This means you can't just affirm without also acting. You have to be disciplined to act and affirm. You have to plant the seeds you want in life. You plant the seeds with your actions, but you water those seeds with your affirmations.

NEGATIVE EMOTIONS

Don't let the past produce the negative emotions of fear, guilt, and anger. So many people have these emotions based on events in their past. It's common to have angry and resentful feelings toward someone based on past experiences. This could be resentment from an ex-spouse, your parents, or past employer. People keep these feelings going years and years after the fact. They want to see these people go through bad things, or they want to try to get back at these people for whatever they did. That's the worst philosophy that you can possibly have. These people continue with their lives doing what they do. Whether they change or not is not your concern. You need to focus on you and your love, your success, your loved ones. The only way you can do this is by forgiving and letting it go.

– Letting Go

Forgive everyone that has done anything wrong to you,

no matter what level of terrible it was. People seem to have this idea that forgiveness is for the person who did the wrongdoing. That's not true. Forgiveness is a selfish act. It allows you to let go of the negative emotions for the sake of your development of love. Forgive. Let it go. 'Holding on to the negative emotions is holding you back from receiving the love you deserve in your life. People aren't evil, but people are capable of doing evil things. Who cares what evil things they do next? Just forgive them for yourself. Then move on.

It's 7 p.m. on a Sunday at LikeMinded church. I walk in and say hi to everyone, as I always do. As I walk to my seat, an usher comes to me and hands me an orange to hold during service. I love this church because the pastor, Justin Sapp, always comes up with innovative ways to resonate with the members.

We go through praise and worship, and Justin begins to preach like normal. The whole time he is speaking, I'm wondering what this orange is for. I'm definitely thinking about eating it. Toward the end of the sermon, he finally asks us to pick up our oranges.

He then tells us how hunters in Africa hunt monkeys to eat. When hunting monkeys, they first get a box and place an orange in it. Then they cut a hole in the box just big enough for the orange to fit through. Eventually, a monkey comes by, sees the orange, and wants to take it out the box. The monkey puts its arm through the hole, grabs the orange, and tries its best to pull the orange out. The problem is the monkey can't pull the orange out because the hole is too small for both the orange and the monkey's paw. All the monkey has to do is let go of the orange to get its paw out. But the monkey stays there making a big ruckus trying to get the orange out the hole for hours sometimes. Then the hunters come along, throw a bag over the monkey, and capture it.

After pastor Sapp tells the story, he has the whole church stand up, grab their oranges, and close their eyes. He then uses the story as an analogy to the things we are holding onto in our lives that are holding us back. The room gets quiet as music plays softly in the background.

He then tells the church: "When you are ready, let the orange go. This orange symbolizes the things that are holding you back from stepping into your destiny." "When you let this orange go, you must also let the thing holding you back go as well." "When you let this orange go it's gone, gone forever."

I hear the deep breaths being taken around the church. Then it happens. The first orange drops. Then the second. After about a minute, all 50 oranges thump the floor. We open our eyes to see multiple people in the church in tears.

This exercise is so powerful. It brings awareness to the

things you realize hold you back. So, what's holding you back? What orange are you holding onto? Will you hold onto it until the hunter comes? Don't go out like a monkey. Let go of the negative emotions. Step into the self-love.

– *Stupid Wall*

We tend to put up this wall when bad things happen to us. Our feelings get hurt, so we hold ourselves back from those who love us. We got cheated in our last deal, so we miss out on the next deal, worried about the possibility of being cheated again. Look, if having courage is one of your values, you can't put up walls to keep out the bad stuff. The same walls you put up to keep the bad stuff out are the same walls that keep the good stuff out. We have to have the courage of being vulnerable even if it can mean being hurt. The side of the wall that has anger, resentment, fear, and hatred is also the place where love, happiness, faith, desire, and hope are. The walls you put up are based on a false perception anyway.

Researchers conducted a study where they took a group of people and counted the number of really bad life-changing experiences they had. Comes to find out that, on the average, a person has only seven terrible life experiences in her entire life. Sure, some more and some less. But don't be overdramatic; the number isn't 30. The question I ask is, if we go through only seven terrible life-changing events, why do we change the way we approach life based on that small number of experience? While thinking about this, 'I realized the walls we put up are stupid. We tend to focus on the bad things, which are very few, and not the good. There are hundreds and thousands of good things that happen to us all the time, but we don't acknowledge them like we should. So, either we focus on the bad or we are poor at math. So, now that you know you're going to go through only seven bad life-changing experiences, what are you going to do about those walls? I suggest you tear them down and live like they were never there.

BEING IN LOVE

Ideal (n.): satisfying one's concept of what is perfect.

Everything I talk about in this book comes from the basic idea—you might say ideal—of becoming a better person. Becoming a better person by cultivating the ideal being inside of us. We can be anything we want to be if we realize that becoming that ideal is the way to do it. Everything we want to do or have are outcomes of who we are.

I often coach people about the love in their relationships. You can tell everything about a person's being based on how they see their relationships. The true test of knowing you can become what you wish is by being in a relationship. If you judge your relationships based on the story you have for the relationship, you are lost to this ideal of being. The 'stories people have about their relationships have nothing to do with true unconditional love. We judge the love based on what the other person does in the relationship instead of just loving the person unconditionally. Love cannot be fully understood; it can only be experienced. The problem is human beings cannot articulate what they are experiencing. Experiences are in the now, and we can never articulate the moment of now. 'Let's test the theory out.

Right now, before you continue reading, think about what you are experiencing now. Take five seconds to experience what you are hearing, thinking, feeling. All right, now go!

If you did the test I just asked you to do, you should realize that you have failed. You failed because when you went to articulate about the experience, it was no longer an experience because it is no longer "now" and longer. It was what you experienced a moment ago. It gets deeper. It wasn't even what you experienced a moment ago because what you experienced a moment ago no longer exist as an experience. It's not an experience any longer. It is now a memory of an experience.

Most people never realize this basic truth. We can live in the now, but we cannot articulate the now. Everything we ever experience turns into a memory of an experience in an instant. This happens because we exist in time, and time is always moving. What does all this have to do with love and being in a relationship? Being in a relationship is an experience; it's not about our past experiences, the 'stories we tell ourselves. When our kids do something that we don't like, we don't make up 'stories about how bad our relationship with our kids is. 'Love between parent and child is unconditional. Do you love unconditionally in your relationships? With true experiencing of a relationship comes true being. If you can be in a relationship, you can be anything, and you can be anything you want with the right concepts of your ideal self.

LOVE AND THE SUCCESSFUL LIFE

When I think of a successful life, I think about having complete congruence with my values. A successful life is not meant to be anything less than 100 percent wholeness in self. A successful life is complete wholeness in the circle of values. Money doesn't matter if you don't have your health. A strong body doesn't matter if your mind is weak. Intelligence doesn't matter if you don't take action. And your religion doesn't matter if you forget to love. Without cultivating all of your values, there will sure to be holes in your life. With holes, we can't be whole.

Life in itself is existence. Love is the general idea of goodwill. Naturally, life must have free will of expression, and love is that very thing, the perfect expression of life. Love is purely the full and unrestricted expression of divine life.

With this idea, I would argue that love is the most important value in creating a successful life. Love is the divine principle that is the driver of all good things. Fear is the opposite of love. This is why fear isn't life. To fear is to express the opposite pole of love. Fear is the root emotion of all bad emotions. Jealousy, envy, and hatred are all negative emotions rooted in fear. If love is the expression of divine life, fear is the expression of limitation. To limit yourself is to be fearful and lack the courage it takes to express love. You cannot have a successful life if you are saturated in fear. The only way to live a successful life is to express yourself at your highest ideals, which is pure love. Love destroys fear and allows your life to match up congruently with your ideals. So, if you can proceed with love, the successful life we all are here to live will appear with great joy.

CHAPTER 8

BELIEF IN A HIGHER AUTHORITY

In 1933, a dictator by the name of Adolf Hitler rose to be the leader of Germany. He took his hatred for a people to drive him to the biggest, most infamous genocide in history. This man led an entire army to kill and torture millions of people. From 1933 to 1945, it is estimated the German army murdered 11 million innocent people, 6 million Jewish. In addition to Jews, the Nazis targeted gypsies, homosexuals, Jehovah's Witnesses, and the disabled for persecution. Hitler sold the Nazis a story about Germans being the best people on earth, and that people who they considered weak should be killed. The torture methods these Germans used were just shocking. They put people's hands in boiling water until their hands and fingernails fell off. They stomped on people's feet with steel-toed boots for minutes at a time. They pressed hot pokers in peoples hands. They hung people from their wrists while they were behind their backs until their shoulders came out of the sockets. They pulled their teeth, cut their ears off, and shocked them with electricity over and over until they died.

I don't believe people are evil, but I do believe people can do really evil things. But how did Hitler get so many people to do all these terrible things? Were all the Nazis just evil people as a whole? Were there really that many people with the same amount of hate as Hitler's, excited to be led to kill? I would say that is not the case. I would argue that these men weren't evil, but they just didn't believe in a higher power. I would argue that none of these men were religious, or if they were, they didn't cultivate the value of spirituality.

Why would people do this to other people? Could you kill?

"Ahhhh, stop!" the learner screams, electricity shocking and going through his body. "Let me out of here. You're hurting me."

The person at the controls, the teacher, looks at the authority figure, realizing he's hurting the learner. "Keep going. The test must go on," the authority figure says in a calm voice.

"Please stop. I told you I have heart problems. My chest hurts," the learner screams.

They are up to about 150 volts now. They started at 15, and the max is 450, which is deadly.

The teacher asks the learner another question, hoping he doesn't get it wrong. The teacher asks the question, but the learner gives an incorrect answer. The teacher puts his head down knowing he's going to have to give this person he just met a mean jolt of electricity. With the authority figure staring at him, telling him to continue, he presses the button. He waits for a reaction, but there is none. The volunteer teacher is extremely nervous. Is he nervous because he is hurting someone? Or is he nervous because he fears getting in trouble?

The authority figure tells him to please continue. The teacher asks what will be the last question he's going to ask the learner today. He asks the question and he gets no reply. He looks at the authority figure, not knowing what to do next.

The authority figure gives him instructions. "If you get no answer, give him a shock anyway."

The teacher gives the authority figure some push-back. "But he's not making any sound. What if he's dead?" the teacher says.

"I'm responsible for this study. Press the button," the authority figure replies.

The volunteer teacher presses the 450- volt button to end the experiment and maybe end a life.

In 1961, Stanley Milgram asked himself the same question I just asked. How could so many people do these horrible things? Are that many people really as evil as we think? Are Germans more obedient than other people? So, Milgram decided to test it out. He put together an experiment at Yale University to see how people would react to an authority figure when they were told to inflict serious harm on another person. This came to be known as Milgram's Obedience experiment.

Milgram used 160 participants in the experiment. Each test in the experiment consisted of two volunteers—a "learner" and a "teacher"—and an authority figure, who was a researcher. One of the volunteers, who always turned out to be the "learner," was an actor. The other volunteer was your average Joe off the streets (all participants were male). The average Joe was the "teacher," and the actor was the "learner." The average Joe did not know that the learner was an actor. He thought he was also a volunteer.

The idea was for the teacher to ask the learner a question, and if he got it right, nothing happened. But if he got it wrong, the teacher had to shock the learner. But, of course, the teachers weren't really shocking the learners. They only thought they were. The researchers told the volunteers that they were testing how people learn with punishment. Each time the learner had to be shocked, the voltage would increase. The machine created volts from 15 all the way up to 450 volts. The 450-volt setting had "XXX" above it to symbolize deadly.

The teacher watched the authority figure tie the learner

to a chair for the test. The teacher then received a shock at 45 volts, just so he could see what it felt like. So, he knew exactly what he was doing to the learner.

The researchers divided the 160 volunteer into four groups of 40. In Group 1, the teacher and the learner were in the same room. When the learner got a question wrong, the teacher had to lift his hand and place it on the machine to give the learner a shock. In Group 2, the learner and the teacher, along with the machine, were in the same room, but the teacher pushed a button separate from the machine that gave the learner a shock. In Group 3, learner and teacher were in separate rooms. The teacher could hear but not see the learner. In Group 4, the teacher and learner were in separate rooms, and the teacher could neither see nor year the learner.

Before the experiment, Milgram estimated what percentage of the volunteers would go through with the whole experiment and seriously harm the learner. The actual statistics in the end were astonishing.

In Group 1 when the teachers had to actually put the learners' hand on the machine, roughly 70 percent of the teachers quit before doing serous harm. That means that 30 percent of Group 1 could actually seriously hurt someone with their hands if someone of authority told them to. In Group 2, 60 percent of the teachers quit before doing serious harm. In Group 4, where the teachers could not hear or see the learner, only 35 percent of the teachers quit, which means that 65 percent of that group thought that they had seriously hurt the learner. When some of the volunteers realized they might be doing serious harm, even killing the learner, all they cared about was their own safety. They asked questions like, am I going to get in trouble for this?

Are you going to get in trouble? Are you kidding me?

These people only cared about themselves and their own safety. They then made excuses for what they did. Excuses like the learner was being stubborn or I had to do what the authority figure told me to. These people had just theoretically hurt, maybe killed, someone and then had the nerve to rationalize it to make themselves feel like they weren't evil. I'm sure if you asked a Nazi soldier why he did those things, he would have said, "Because I was ordered to."

Milgram believed you can't ask people what they would do in a situation, but you have to just put them in the situation to see what they would do. I'm sure if he asked those people could they hurt or even kill someone before the experiment, their answer, of course, would have been no. But guess what? They did.

I can't put you in that situation, but I'll ask you the questions. Would you have stopped when you realized you were almost killing someone? Would you have stopped even though the authority figure told you to keep going, knowing what you were doing was wrong? Would you have leaned on the excuse that it's not my responsibility? I'm just following orders? Are you just an obedient follower in your flesh, or do you believe in a higher code? Can you kill?

BELIEF IN A HIGHER AUTHORITY

Let's talk about the people who didn't go through with the entire Milgram experiment. What was so different about these people and the people who "seriously hurt" or even "killed" the learner? These people stopped when they realized they were hurting another human being. These people didn't listen to authority because they knew what they were doing was wrong. The people who didn't go all the way believed in a higher power. They believed in an authority above all authorities. These people were not necessarily religious, but they all believed in a higher moral code. They believed in the authority above man and felt accountable to the authority of their spirituality.

'I believe if you do not cultivate the value of spirituality, you could also kill. The reason is if you don't abide by a higher code, you are submissive and obedient. Martin Luther King, Jr., believed in a higher code and used his gift of communication to bring it to this world. If God says we are all created equal, then, dammit, we should live like that on earth. If you don't believe in a higher power, then most likely you would follow someone, even if they lead you to kill.

SOW TO THE SPIRIT

"Whoever sows to please their flesh, from the flesh will reap destruction; whoever sows to please the Spirit, from the Spirit will reap eternal life" (Galatians 6:8, NIV). That verse says everything I know about cultivating spirituality in just a few words. You reap what you sow is a small but major concept we all, for the most part, know about. This means whatever you put your energy into, you are going to get back results based on what that energy does. If you plant orange seeds, you will get an orange tree. If you plant weeds, you will get weeds.

He who sows to the flesh gets corruption. When the Bible talks about the flesh, it talks about our sinful selves. The flesh is the reactive part of our being. The flesh wants to gratify ourselves and doesn't care about others. The flesh is the birthplace of anger, resentment, jealousy, hatred, and all the negative emotions that we harbor. If we plant weeds, we will get weeds back. What this verse is saying is that if you plant to the flesh, you will get corruption. Just as Hitler sowed to his fleshly beliefs of the Aryan people—that's corruption at its best, or worst!

3 Steps to Reap the Good Things in Life
1. Plant the value of spirituality.
2. Plant the things in life that really matter.
3. Sow to the spirit and reap everlasting life.

– Spirit Versus Flesh
We talked about what the spirit is, and we talked about

what the flesh is. We also talked about the power of sowing and reaping these two entities. What we have not discussed is the everlasting battle between these two entities. There is a never-ending battle between the flesh and the spirit taking place inside of us. As it says in Galatians 5:17: " "For the flesh desires what is contrary to the Spirit, and the Spirit what is contrary to the flesh. They are in conflict with each other, so that you are not to do whatever you want" (NIV).

It's a battle between the good and the evil within us. It's a constant day-to-day, minute-to-minute battle. So, who's going to win your internal battles? I don't know about you, but I'm competitive. I will not lose this battle. We aren't in competition with anyone else. We are in competition with ourselves.

Michael Jordan, the best basketball player to ever play the game, said it best. A journalist asked him, "How do you stay on top? How do you continue to get better when you are the best?"

"Everyone is in competition with me," Michael replied. "But I'm in competition with myself,"

He understood that nobody could stop him, only himself. The same thing goes for all of us. We are in a battle with ourselves. The secret weapon to this internal battle is discipline. So, arm yourself with the self-control of discipline and use its power to win the battle of your mind.

– *Feeding the Beast*

"My son, there is a battle between two wolves inside all of

us. One is evil. It is anger, jealousy, greed, resentment, inferiority, lies, and ego. The other is good. It is joy, peace, love, hope, humility, kindness, empathy, and truth," the elder said.

The little boy thought about it. "Grandfather, which one of the wolves wins?" he asked.

The old man looked at his grandson and softly said, "The one you feed."

We are capable of great, and we are capable of evil. We all have evil thoughts as well as great thoughts. The key is to have the discipline to feed the right beast. That is the point of this Cherokee fable. Which beast are you feeding? Are you feeding the evil beast, or are you feeding the good beast? These rhetorical questions I'm asking are my attempts to get you to realize one truth, the truth that you have a choice to feed the beast you want to. You have the choice to choose good over evil. It's a matter of focusing on the good, cultivating the good, and feeding the right beast.

– *The Boring Superhero*

When I was growing, my siblings and I were really into comic books. We had them all from Batman to Superman to the X-Men. What made these 'superheroes so appealing, besides the fact that they had amazing powers? What made the stories so appealing that these comics now are billion dollar movies? I would argue the reason is because of the villains. Who would Batman be without the Joker, Bain, and Two Face? Who would Superman be without Lex Luther and Kryptonite? Think of how boring Superman would be if there were no such thing as Kryptonite, if in every episode there was nothing that could give Superman a hard time and bring the story to climax. What if Superman had no tough challenges and he could just destroy Lex Luther without trying, would you still watch? Of course not. What makes superheroes so amazing is the hard times they go through and their ability to overcome them.

This is what life is about. Without the conflict of opposites, life is boring. How can you be proud and enjoy your successes if you have nothing to overcome? Positive and negative, good and evil, life and death, health and illness, light and dark, winning and losing—it makes for a great journey. The journey is what makes Superman so appealing. You can't triumph if you have no obstacles to surpass. Superman owes all of his fame to the same thing that hurts him the most. Without Kryptonite, superman would be a boring superhero.

MY POINT

Even though I am Christian, I read and learn about all types of faiths. I don't do a deep dive into them, but I know enough to be somewhat knowledgeable. That's why in this chapter I talk about spirituality, not just Christianity. It's not about just what I believe; it's also about what you believe and what others believe. Whatever that belief is, cultivate it. "Thinking outside the box" is impossible, although people use the quote so much. Your box is the accumulation of everything you know. So how can you think outside the box if your perspective isn't broad? This is why I learn about other religions and others' views on spirituality'. I believe in love for all human beings regardless of where they are from or what they believe in. I seek exposure to different views and concepts so I can expand my thinking (my box). If your exposure is limited, your box is limited. We tend to judge the things

Cultivate your beliefs, but also respect the beliefs of others. And never forget to love everyone.

we do not understand. So, I seek understanding of different perspectives so that I won't judge, and I can love on everyone.

All religions have their differences, of course, but a lot of the major values are the same. For example, love is at the forefront of all religions. Look at the last three sections I wrote in this book. They all explain the same idea but with different illustrations. "Spirit Versus Flesh," "Feeding the Beast," and "The Boring Superhero" are all the same ideas in a different package. Spirit versus the flesh is from the Bible. The story of the wolves is a Native American story. And the illustration about 'superheroes is my own. I'm positive we could look at all religions and find similar stories to illustrate the same lessons. When you look at most spiritual' systems broadly, you see they teach the same divine messages.

– *Study, Practice, Preach*

For anything you truly believe in and are passionate about, you must learn it, practice, it, and teach it on a frequent basis. Your faith is the deepest value that is close to your heart. This is why when we get in deep conversation about religion, it can lead and build up to a huge argument. This is what we deeply believe. How dare somebody say it's wrong? Dialogues about religion, in my opinion, are healthy. I believe the value of our religion is worth protecting with all of our heart, without falling into anger. All values must be protected, but the value of your spiritual beliefs must be protected most strongly. I believe daily we should follow certain disciplines that cultivate these values. Such discipline not only makes your value stronger but also prepares you for any dialogue you engage in.

THE SCRIPT OF LIFE

Let's do a little exercise using imagination. Really quick—now!

Imagine that you are a world-famous actor, like a Denzel Washington, but even better. One day you get a call inviting you to an audition. You get to the audition and the director doesn't need you to audition; you got the part. You were made for this part. You are the absolute perfect person for the job. You show up to the set early to get ready. You get your makeup done. The set is ready. Everything is ready. You are in the perfect position for the best and biggest movie of your career. You walk on set and get into place, and the director yells out, "Action!" Then you realize there is a big problem. Everything is perfectly in place, but you're missing the most importance piece. You don't have the script.

You were so hyped up to start this groundbreaking role you didn't even think to ask or look for the script. You didn't prepare yourself by studying the script, as all the best actors do.

I am Christian, so naturally I believe my script is the Bible. In the movie of life, I believe the Bible is the script we must live in congruence with to achieve the cultivation of anything. If you want to crush this movie role, pick up your script and make sure you know it so that you are ready for this big movie role we call life.

4 Questions About Your Script

1. Are you studying the script of life?
2. Are you studying what you believe a life script is so that you know how to play this movie role we call life?
3. Do you read your Bible daily?
4. If it's the script of life, why 'don't you?

I DON'T SEE WHAT YOU SEE

I had a small debate about studying the Bible with a friend of mine recently. I was explaining to her that you should read your Bible every day for yourself. She began to argue that she doesn't want to get the wrong meaning of things in the Bible, so she goes to church for the preacher to articulate it to her. She had a valid argument, it seemed, but there was a problem with it. What I read, what I hear, and what I see is different than what you read, hear, or see. We can look at the exact same thing but see something different. We can read the exact same words and take away different meanings. What I hear may be something different from what your may hear. This is the reason why the game of telephone rarely works.

In the game of telephone, you line up multiple people and try to keep a message the same. You tell one person a message and hope that person articulates the message to the next person and the next person until the last person gets the message. The goal is to have the exact message word for word in the end. If you've ever played this game, you know it rarely happens.

I told my friend that what she reads is different from what the pastor reads. How the verse resonates with her may be different from how it resonates with the pastor. This is one reason why I believe the Bible is written in parables. We all get from the word what we need for ourselves. Saying that everyone gets the same meaning from every chapter and verse is like saying we all should have the same prayers. Read the Bible, or whatever your religion has, and see what it says to you. Allow the great wisdom of it to resonate to the point you make your own meaning. Be a student, not a follower. Read it, learn it, and make your own decisions based on how it talks to you. This is one reason why hate gets spread into the world. People listen to a preacher's interpretation of a scripture and feel it's the right interpretation even if it involves hate. I'm not saying don't listen to your pastor, nor am I preacher bashing. All I'm saying is get the information yourself and make your own decisions. At the end of the day, you have to live with the results.

PRACTICE

Now that you have the information and you are in daily study, you have to practice. When I say "practice," I don't mean rolling the basketball out to work on your jumper. I mean to act in congruence with your beliefs. Someone once said that we must say and do the things we actually believe because the things we say and do are the symbols of who we are. Let's look into this a little bit deeper.

When I read that quote, the word that jumps into my mind is integrity. Integrity is doing the right thing even when nobody is looking. Integrity is acting in congruence with your beliefs because it's your value, not because people are looking. Your values are the deepest roots of who you are. So, you must live in line with these values so that you attract the things, people, and results in your life that you want. So that you can become a Success Magnet™. Remember, if you plant oranges, you will get oranges. Same goes with practicing what you believe in. The saying, "Practice what you preach," is a little outdated. Let that saying now read, "Practice what you believe." If we practice what we believe, we will reap what we generally want in life. When we practice what we believe, we become Godlike.

NATURE'S BALANCE

I believe that human beings are made specifically in a way to have complete control over the earth. I believe that we were tailor-made to be able to conquer anything if we really want to. Nature upholds a balance, and we are made to fit perfectly in that balance. The theory of evolution is the idea that animals change over time to fit this balance. It's not a coincidence that we naturally fit this balance to perfection. But the only way to live in this balance is to cultivate our values.

THE RAS

I want to give you one example of many that proves we are made to uphold nature's balance. There is a law of nature called the law of attraction. The law of attraction is the idea that whatever you focus on the most will manifest. So, if you focus on the good things in life, good will come to you. If you focus on the bad, the bad will come. The law of attraction says, "If you focus on what you want, and have resolve to achieve it, the universe will mold and move in your favor." Whether you believe this law is true or not is irrelevant to the point I'm about to make. I do believe in this law and that we have something in our brains that communicates with this law.

At the base of our brains is something called the reticular activating system, also known as the RAS filter. The RAS filter filters out anything that's not important to us. We receive millions and billions of bits of information constantly. The RAS filter screens out what we don't feel is important so that we don't get overwhelmed by the constant intake of information. It's like in the latest Superman movie.

Superman, in the latest movie, had a problem filtering out all the voices in the world. He had superhearing powers, so he was getting bombarded with voices until he learned to quiet the noise. The same thing would happen to us if we didn't have the reticular activating system. If you're in a big room full of thousands of people, and someone calls your name, you can still hear that amongst all the noise. That's your RAS filter in action. It filtered out all the noise and pulled out your name, which of course is important to you.

This part of the brain works in congruence with the law of attraction to attract the things we want in life. This filter allows us to focus and use the law of attraction to attain what we wish. I'll prove it. Do you have a dream car? You know, that car that you would buy if you had the money to get it. Think about how and when the car became your dream car. Now you see the car all of the time. It could be a $300,000 car, but you happen to see that car all the time because it's your dream car. This is because when it became your dream car, it set into your RAS filter. You told yourself that the car was important, so now your RAS filter notices its look, sound, and even smell.

My good friend Brandon can hear a car and tell you what kind of car it is before he even sees it. He can't do this with your basic Honda Civic, but he can do it with a Lamborghini. He can't do this because he's a supercar enthusiast, but he can do this because it's set into his RAS filter. So, to focus our RAS filter on our goals, all we have to do is write them down. There are other ways to do this, but this is the easiest way. When we write our goals down, we actually place what we want in our RAS filter, which works with the law of attraction to bring it to us. This universe is governed by laws, and we have perfect systems to live in congruence with these laws. The RAS filter is only one of the many examples of this idea.

IN HIS IMAGE

> Then God said, Let us make mankind in our image, in our likeness, so that they may rule over the fish in the sea and the birds in the sky, over the livestock and all the wild animals, and over all the creatures that move along the ground. (Genesis 1:26, NIV)

If you believe in God and the Bible, that's a powerful

and exciting verse. It implies that the idea I have about us being perfectly fit for the world's laws is absolutely true. I believe the only way to tap into this power is to cultivate our values. Think about it—human civilization has come such a long way. We have done things and will do things that are flat out remarkable. The Creator has given us this power to tap into. All we have to do is learn it, live by it, and pay it forward. We are meant to be great. We are kings and queens amongst this earth. God is the king of kings and the king of queens, not the king of mediocrity. So, go and get your crown. The only way to claim your crown is to know who you are, which is a king or queen, then build your values correctly. God gave us the power, Godlike power, and sent us His only son to make sure we kept that power. That's love.

As it says in Corinthians 6:19-20:

> "Do you not know that your bodies are temples of the Holy Spirit, who is in you, whom you have received from God? You are not your own; you were bought at a price. Therefore honor God with your bodies" (NIV).

As humans, our greatest error in life is to have the power of God and not use it. Jesus paid the price of His non-sinful life because He loved us so much. The last part says our spirits are gods. So make sure you sow into the spirit because your spirit is a God. We are Godlike. God said it. Believe it, and it is done!

THE PERFECT MENTOR

Imagine having a mentor that is perfect in every way. Someone who knows everything and could tell you exactly what to do to progress. What if you had someone smarter than Albert Einstein, richer than Bill Gates, and more powerful than any world leader telling you what to do? Well, this is the power you can have if you let God be your mentor. You might ask, how can I allow God to mentor me and talk to me? All you have to do is learn to listen. Learn to soak in silence, and allow Him to speak to you.

To let someone mentor you, you must first have a relationship with that person. In a healthy relationship, the two parties have to communicate. Talk to God with prayer every day. Sit in silence and let Him speak to you. Ask Him questions. Sit still in silence so that He can speak to you. This can sound weird if you don't have a relationship with God already. But trust me; He wants to talk to you just as much as you want Him to mentor you. He has a destiny for you to complete. All you have to do is listen intentionally so that He can tell you what that destiny is. In the Bible, when God came to speak to people, most of the time they were in silent places, and they were listening. If you want that relationship with Him as badly as He wants one with you, all you have to do is talk to Him and listen to Him.

THE DOOR TO THE SOUL

Our souls are the very thing that will improve our outer life. We must work on our souls and cultivate them. "As within so without." The inside always manifests on the outside. We can't see with our physical eyes what is going on inside. That is the reason so many people feel they must chase things on the outside. They chase after what they see. But the law reads, "As within so without," not "as without so within." The key is to work on the inside; the outside will follow. By looking inwardly, we can open the door to the soul. We cannot open this door outward because it only opens inward. Everything outside that you lust for will only come from the inside.

− *The Test*

Nothing can be helped from the outside. Even God does not help us from the outside. God works from within us. Nothing can be saved or destroyed from the outside either. The outside is an expression of the inside. That's why it kills me when people say, "God is testing me." God does not need to test you. He already knows everything. It is us who need to learn, not God. Every struggle or test we have was brought on by ourselves. We go through problems because we aren't living a congruent life. The true test is to live in the present, in congruence with our highest ideals. When we take the leap to live in congruence with the actual ideal we have for ourselves, something amazing happens. The test is passed with flying colors, and the demonstration of your success comes to life.

But if we aren't tested, why do things go wrong? Things go wrong because of our false beliefs. We've all heard the famous Bible verse "Though I walk through the valley of the shadow of death." Notice this statement does not say death; it says the "shadow of death." The shadow of our false beliefs. There is no death, only the false belief in such. False beliefs that you have to chase the things you want to attain. False beliefs that you are not able to reach your highest ideals. False beliefs that there is a shortcut in achieving success. You would never have the desire to be successful if there were not potential to be successful. The reason most people don't achieve the success they want is because they chase aimlessly to catch it. This is just the opposite of the concept of the Success Magnet™.

> But the key to success in one sentence is this:
> We must make ourselves ready for the things we want most.

– *100 Percent Responsibility*

I invite you to do something that 99 percent of people will never do. It could be from ignorance or from fear, but people never want to take full responsibility for their own life. If you dare to do this, I'm going to show you the power that comes with it.

We perceive things the way we want to perceive them. If you take responsibility for your perceptions, you can be the cause in your life and create the effect you want. The universal law of cause and effect says "every effect has a cause." We are the cause, and what we think, say, and believe creates an effect. This is the truth whether you know it and accept it or not.

The Bible (New International Version) teaches this truth in the first three verses.

- ❖ Genesis 1:1—"In the beginning God created the heavens and the earth." (The universal law of cause and effect.)
- ❖ Genesis 1:2—"Now the earth was formless and empty, darkness was over the surface of the deep." (There is no effect without a cause.)
- ❖ Genesis 1:3—"And God said, 'Let there be light,' and there was light." (This is where the magic happens, where the effect is created.)

I don't wish to force any beliefs on you, but it seems to me these three verses explain not only how the universe was created but also how we create our own universe here on earth. What we think, what we say, and what we strongly believe create an effect, and we were the cause. The point I want you to get is when you take full 100 percent responsibility for your life, you can then harness this power and become the god under God that you were meant to be.

CHAPTER 9

THE VALUE BRIDGE

I've shared the ideas and values that helped me go from being broke to where I am today. I hope I was able to educate you and inspire you to cultivate these major values. But I would be doing a disservice to you if I didn't give you the ideas that build the bridge to success. The bridge that took me from nothing to something. The bridge that leads to anywhere you want to go. You don't cross this bridge so that you can find success. You build the bridge so that success can come to you. It's another way to help you become a Success Magnet™. You might ask, so, Roy, how do you build this bridge? Let's talk about it.

THE FOUNDATION

The foundation and the absolutely most important attribute you need to cultivate your values is discipline. Discipline is the key to all success. Everybody wants some sexy secret to achieving what they want, but there is none. The truth is it's not sexy one bit, and it takes pure discipline. It takes the discipline to read the books. It takes the discipline to work out, to eat right, to meditate, to do all the things that will help you progress. Now that you have the knowledge, place the discipline in your everyday life. Get it done. No excuses.

We are what we do every day. So, the key is to discipline ourselves to build the transformational habits it takes to improve ourself. People think that highly successful people have some secret to attaining everything they have. That's not true at all. I don't know if people really believe that, or if they tell themselves that so they don't have to face the facts. The fact that is they will have to dig down and become a disciplined person.

Kobe Bryant didn't just come out of the womb one of the best players ever. No. He's worked his butt off every day since he was three years old. Discipline, discipline, discipline.

THE COMPOUND EFFECT

Darren Hardy wrote a book that helped me tremendously. It's a book on discipline. The idea of the book is that small disciplines done every day compounded over time creates momentum, and that momentum leads to the success you want. On the flip side, if you don't discipline yourself, the compound effect will work in a negative way. Small bad judgments compounded over time lead to failure. Small judgments like not saving money, not paying attention to the details, and not living right is why I ended up broke pushing my car on the freeway. It sucked to tell myself that is was my fault, but it was essential for my growth.

OUR TRUE CLOTHING

I have a little secret many don't know about when it comes to becoming disciplined. Becoming a highly disciplined person seems hard because people go about it in the wrong way. Becoming disciplined is fairly easy. All you have to do is create the habits needed to succeed. There are thousands of self-help books that talk about how to build habits. Most of them talk about forcing the habit until you get used to doing it. They say something like "work it for 30 days, and it will become a habit." Look, success is God's gift. He has made it simple for us to achieve. God is the Creator. We are made in His image, which makes us creators. All you have to do is create the ideal you want and then become that ideal. When you do this, you will see how easy it is to be successful.

Don't try to force a habit. Instead, make your own self-image through becoming better, and the habit will follow.

To tell you the truth, limiting yourself is harder than being successful. When I made six figures, it was easier than what I did to become broke, embarrassed, and heartbroken. The problem was I was ignorant—even worse, I didn't know I was ignorant, so I was blind. All I had to do was create the ideal and become that ideal.

The original meaning of the word habit is "garment" or "a piece of clothing." As you know, different people dress differently. A basketball player dresses differently than a soccer player. A lawyer dresses differently than a doctor. An adult dresses differently than a child. The type of clothing we wear is based on the type of person we are, or the image we have for ourselves. Our clothes fit us. So, if a habit of working out were a shirt, who does the person who puts on that shirt look like? If reading as a habit were some shoes, what does a person who reads look like? Look at the habit you want as a article of clothing and ask yourself, who dresses like this? We are our habits. Our habits are the clothing that we wear.

TRANSFORM

You'll notice that most of the ideas in this book are transformational disciplines. There is a difference between transactional tasks and transformational tasks. Transactional tasks are the doing. Transformational tasks are the becoming. You can do a bunch of transactional chores to chase your dreams, but it will never make you the person you need to be to achieve those dreams. Transformational tasks stretch you and your abilities so that you transform into a better person. I'm not saying don't do transactional things, but what I am saying is don't skip the transformational things that will change your life.

BEING

We are human beings, not human doings. That is why you can't rely on what you do to chase success. You must focus on who you are becoming so that you can become a Success Magnet™. Success doesn't respond to what you do; it responds to who you are. Once you realize and embrace this fact, I promise your life will change. When I hit rock bottom, there was nothing I could do to fix it. But I could become the person I needed to be so that it would fix itself. Things come into our life based on what we attract. We are all magnets, but what kind of magnet are you? To find that out, all you have to do is look at what is being drawn into your life. If you're not drawing into your life what you want, don't think about what you can do to fix it, but rather change who you are becoming.

Don't focus on doing more. Instead, focus on becoming more. Then what you want will magically appear.

IT'S CHOICE TIME

Choose now. Choose to discipline yourself to make your values strong. Choose to step into your purpose. 'Don't wait to choose when all your ducks are lined up. Your ducks will never be lined up! A choice is made somewhere between zero to five seconds. I challenge you to choose now. Are you going to settle? Or are you going to take what's yours?

– Be a Tree

A tree grows as tall as it possibly can no matter what happens. A tree does not have a choice. It's going to grow as tall as it can—period. Every tree you have ever seen grows to its maximum potential, no exceptions. I'm asking you to be like a tree. I'm asking you to choose to grow to your highest potential. How tall can you honestly grow? You will never know until you discipline yourself and cultivate your values to the max.

– Dignity of Choice

So, if a tree grows to its maximum potential, why don't we grow to our maximum potential? The paradox about being human is we can choose to create our own path. We have the ability and the dignity to make our own decisions. A tree cannot do this. A tree doesn't have a choice. You are not a tree. God called us to be obedient, but He did not force us to be obedient. He gave us the ability to decide for ourselves. He gave us the dignity of choice. Freedom isn't having the ability to cultivate your values, but freedom is having the willingness to cultivate your values. So choose to be the best you can be, and make Him proud, make yourself proud.

APPLY IT

I can give you ideas and ways to cultivate your values,

but only you can apply them to your life. I can't tell you to read from 10 p.m. to 11 p.m. every night like I do because you have a different schedule than I have. You have to look at your own schedule and manage your time and energy. You have to use your own expression to apply it to your life. The acquiring of knowledge isn't wisdom, but wisdom is the ability to apply that knowledge to your own life. You can read all the books in the world, but if you can't apply what you read, it means nothing.

4 Steps for Applying Anything to Your Life

1. Study: Study whatever it is you want or need to know. Grab a few books on the subject and read them. Grab some audiotapes that teach the subject as well. Also find someone who is familiar with the subject.

2. Capture: Capture the knowledge so that you will remember it and be able to find it easily. Write down in your journal the best ideas you have learned and revisit them.

3. Act: Implement the ideas into your life. Knowledge without action is wasted. Knowledge is not power; knowledge is only potential power. Act on that knowledge.

4. Check results: Check the results of the disciplines that you have implemented. Look to see if they working. Don't waste your time on something that doesn't bring you results.

CHAPTER 10

THE TIME IS NOW

In this book, we have talked about everything it takes to make yourself better. We took a deep dive into each value that I feel is important to everyone. Sure, there are other values in life besides the five I've stressed. But these are the five major ones that took me from broke to six figures in 24 short months. I'm not the smartest person. I just realized through study that there are certain values successful people worked on to attract success, to become Success Magnets™. They all cultivated these values because they knew the importance of themselves. They understood that chasing society's standard of success would get them nowhere fast. Instead, they worked on their own values so that they could attract success and achieve the future ideals they had of themselves.

THE TRUTH

The truth about success is it's not a destination. The key

to life is progression. There is no end in life, but every end is a beginning. We all have an inner drive for challenge, no matter how successful we are. The outcome of that challenge is progress. Progress is the key to true happiness. A person can have a lot of success, but he won't be happy if he 'doesn't continue to improve. If we achieve a goal, yes, we are successful. But after achieving that goal, we must set new goals. After we achieve a future ideal, we then have to strive for another future ideal. If success is not a destination, how can you chase it?

3 More Definitions of Success
1.   Success is something you become.
2.   Success is a never-ending process of achieving future ideals through progression.
3.   Success is who you are and who you become.

WHAT FIRST?

I've shared many of my ideas and directives that have helped me attain the success I've had. You're probably asking yourself, what do I do first? I know all this info can be a little much to take in and apply, but you have to start somewhere. Please don't put this book down and think too much about what you should do. Get started. Take the value most important to you, and start a discipline. If it's loving your spouse, find out her love language and start speaking that language to her daily. If it's gaining more wisdom, purchase some books and read them. Add the disciplines to your life now! So, What's your most important value? Identify it and start. One discipline affects all disciplines, so once you start, you'll be on your way to becoming a Success Magnet™.

THIS WORKS

Once you determine what is your most important value and get the discipline, you'll find many opportunities to put it to the test.

It's my off day, and I'm relaxing when my phone rings. I don't want to answer it. But I look at the number and see it's a good friend. Why is she calling me? I pick up and all I hear is crying on the other end. I want to ask what's wrong, but I stay present and just listen. My good friend and coworker, Lindsey, tells me that a friend of ours wants to kill himself. I just hung out with him the other day, so I didn't believe it. He seemed fine. She tells me that he's depressed and told her how he's going to kill himself. Lindsey is one of those people who has a big loving heart and is there for everybody. I assure her everything will be OK and tell her to calm down. Based on the tone of her voice, I can tell she is really concerned and scared for our friend's life. Our friend, John, has had a lot of hardships in his life, especially around the time of this incident. Lindsey asks me to hang around John as much as I can so that he 'doesn't hurt himself. I call up John and ask him does he want to hang out.

Several days later, John comes over to my apartment and we start to just dialogue about life. John 'doesn't want to tell me how he is feeling inside, but I realize something is wrong. I start to think about how I could help John through what he is going through. He's a really prideful guy and doesn't like to admit he is doing badly. I invite him to church, but he 'doesn't believe in God. So, I decide to invite John to participate in all of my daily disciplines with me. I invite him to work out with me and my good friend, Jeff, every day. Every day we run at the beach and discuss our visions and dreams.

We do this for a month straight, and I see a dramatic change in John. He is in better shape, has made a vision for himself, and starts making progress in his life. John wants to be a police officer but doesn't believe he can be because of a past incident on his record. Jeff tells him after one or our running sessions, "John, through God anything is possible."

John respects Jeff so he actual begins to listen and believe in God. The next day Jeff calls me and tells me he had a dream that John was a police officer. My friends and I put a meaning behind everything. We don't believe things just happen. We believe there is a reason for everything.

The next day John calls me and says he needs to see me immediately. I meet with him at my apartment, anxious about what is going on. When I see him, he has tears coming down his face, not bad tears, but tears of joy. I ask him what's going on, and he hits me with it. "Bro, I got a police job in Chicago," he says. "I just confirmed a hour ago."

I gave him a big hug as he cries. He tells me there has to be a God because this is impossible.

"Nothing's impossible, bro," I tell him. "Just give Him thanks and understand He loves you."

John then tells me how I saved his life. He tells me that he had a plan and a set time to kill himself just a month prior. He says the only reason he didn't do it is because I invited him to come work out with me. "Thank you, Roy. Thank you," he says.

I hug him tighter. "Thank God, bro, not me."

To this day, John is doing great. He works in a police job and is well on his way to the vision he built for himself. Just something as small as exercise and being around people who want the best for him turned his life around. It turned his life around from wanting to kill himself to his working in dream job in just a couple months. You can't change your life in and instant, but you can change your direction immediately.

BEING RIGHT VERSUS BEING SUCCESSFUL

Right now, you are judging this book. You are judging the

ideas. You are judging the author. And you are juxtaposing the content to what you already know. You may be thinking this book was written poorly or expertly. You might be thinking the ideas in this book make sense or 'are total nonsense. It's OK to judge because that's what we naturally do as humans. But there is a difference between being right and being successful. I do not care about being right about my ideas. I only care about your success. I don't know your level of success, but I want you to make this very important distinction: "people would rather be right than be successful."

This seems to be the No. 1 human drive. Humans care about protecting their identity more than anything else. We desperately care about protecting our identity in the eyes of society. We desire success and results so strongly because they make us right. Success is the ultimate proof of being right, hands down. We all argue, we all make good points about our concepts, but when you can share results, there is no higher proof that you are right. Becoming successful makes you, without any doubt, right about what you believe.

I've worked in the medical field for a decade, and I see this all the time. People would rather be right about their pain, their sickness, and their disabilities than getting rid of them. This is why placeboes work in medicine. A placebo is a fake medicine, and that fake medicine rids some people of their symptoms. There have been plenty of studies on this principle, yet scientists don't know why placeboes work. It seems to me that they work because they allow people to be right about their pain. The mind is extremely powerful, and whatever concepts we have about ourselves dictate that power. A lot of success gurus sell the idea that you should stop trying to be right and care only about results. That's not a bad idea. It will change the quality of 'your life for the better. But it's such a powerful human drive it leaves you trying to fight it your whole life instead of harnessing it. When I was pushing my car in the cold—broke, depressed, and embarrassed—I received a powerful gift, the gift of responsibility. With the gift of responsibility, I was able to harness the power of trying to be right instead of avoiding it.

THE GIFT OF SELF-EFFICACY

If I can give you the principle of success in one word, that word would be self-efficacy. Taking total responsibility for your own life truly makes you a Success Magnet™. There is a ton of books on this, and they are all amazing in articulating this gift, but they all articulate it in a way that makes it really difficult to get it done. I am going to give you the secret to using the gift of responsibility in an easy but extremely powerful way.

We said that the biggest human drive is to be right. The key is to use the gift of self-efficacy with this human drive to be right. Start changing your language and calling forth the person you wish to be. That's why my favorite book says, "Call those things that be not, as if they are." The ultimate statement in becoming what you wish always starts with I am. You must say what you are, as if you are already that. I am (followed by what you wish to be.) When you do this, you will feel the power of the statement shoot through your body. It's such an amazing thing. I am. The mind wants to protect your identity, which makes your No. 1 drive to be right about what you are. Affirming who you are with I am, allows you to use the gift of responsibility to bring that statement into being. The mind only wants to be right, so when you say you are something, the mind goes to work to make what you said right. When people say I am sick, their mind goes to work to keep them right, so they become sick. Remember, God made this universe with words, so be careful what words you speak. But if you say the words I am with intention to what you wish to be, you will be and become whatever you create.

THE TIME IS NOW

I hope you weren't looking for some sexy secret on how to bring success to you. The truth is it takes discipline and hard work. But would you feel successful if it were so easy to do? If it were easy, everyone would do it, right? The fact that it's not easy should excite you. Excite you because when you become a Success Magnet™, you step into a realm that most can't achieve. You have greatness inside of you that I hope this book brings out. Discipline added in with proper recovery is the key to all improvement.

We human beings are like a gold nugget in raw form. When you find gold in its raw form, it is not yet the shiny gold that we see. It has to be refined and broken down with fire before you bring out its true value. We are the same way. Before you can bring out the shiny person in you, we have to be refined with discipline, hard work, and personal development. Don't let your lizard brain make excuses why the philosophies in this book won't serve you. The lizard wants you to be comfortable. But I'm calling on you to become uncomfortable. I'm calling on you to step out of that comfort and step into your destiny.

God didn't put success somewhere and tell you to go get it. He has already blessed you with success if you would just live in congruence with your highest ideals. When you start your journey, you will falter, but just regather and keep going. Anything with any longevity gets off course, but the key is to align back with your values and keep pushing. Believe in your abilities.

You have complete control over who you become. You have complete dominion over everything in this world if you would just sharpen the tools God has given you.

Believe in your values. Believe in yourself. I hope this book resonates with you and makes you realize your own greatness. All you have to do is when you put this book down, is to pick up the disciplines and become a Success Magnet™.

I truly believe in the message in this book. These simple principles changed my whole life. If this book served you in any way, please serve someone else and pass it on to them.

For a free coaching session email Roy at roy@royredd.com.

BIBLIOGRAPHY

- Aristotle. Nicomachean Ethics. 350 B.C.
  Translated by W.D. Ross.

- Bible Hub. *www.biblehub.com.*

- Breuning, Loretta Graziano.
  I, Mammal: Why Your Brain Links Status and Happiness.
  Oakland: System Integrity Press, 2011.

- Breuning, Loretta Graziano.
  Meet Your Happiness Chemicals.
  Oakland: System Integrity Press, 2012.

- Burchard, Brendon.
  The Charge: Activating the 10 Human Drives That Make You Feel Alive.
  New York: Free Press, 2012.

- Bureau of Labor Statistics of the U.S. Department of Labor. *Customer Price Index.*
  Washington D.C. www.bls.gov, 2013.

- Chapmen, Gary D. *The 5 Love Languages: How to Express Heartfelt Commitment to Your Mate.*
  Chicago: NorthField Publishing, 1992.

- Clason, George S. *The Richest Man in Babylon.*
  New York: Signet, 2002.

- Centers for Disease Control. *Adult Obesity Facts.* Atlanta, GA: www.cdc.gov, 2012.

- DeMarco, M.J. *The Millionaire Fastlane: Crack the Code of Wealth and Live Rich for a Lifetime.* Phoenix: Viperion Publishing Corp, 2011.

- Durant, Will, & Durant, Ariel. *The Lessons of History.* New York: Fine Communications, 1997.

- Hanh, Thich N. *Being Peace.* Berkeley: Parallax Press, 1988.

- Hardy, Darren. *The Compound Effect: Jump-start Your Income, Your Life, Your Success.* Kettering, OH: Success Books, 2010.

- "Ideal." *The Oxford College Dictionary.* www.oxforddictionaries.com/us/definition/american_english/, 2002.

- Milgrim, Stanley. *Obedience to Authority: An Experimental View.* New York: Harper Perennial, 2009.

- Mull, Brandon. *FableHaven.* Salt Lake City: Shadow Mountain, 2006.

- "Potential." *The Oxford American College Dictionary.* www.oxforddictionaries.com/us/definition/american_english/, 2002.

- Rand, Ayn. *Atlas Shrugged.*
  New York: Plume, 1999.

- Ratey, John, & Hagerman, Eric. Spark:
  The Revolutionary New Science of Exercise and the Brain.
  New York: Little, Brown and Company, 2013.

- "Results." *The Oxford American College Dictionary.*
  www.oxforddictionaries.com/us/definition/
  american_english/, 2002.

- "Religion." *The Oxford American College Dictionary.*
  www.oxforddictionaries.com/us/definition/
  american_english/, 2002.

- Robbins, Tony. *Why We Do What We Do.*
  New York: www.Ted.com, 2006.

- Rohn, James E. *How to Have Your Best Year Ever.*
  Kettering, OH: Jim Rohn International, 1993.

- Rohn, James E. *The Art of Exceptional Living.*
  Kettering, OH: Jim Rohn International, 1993.

- Rohn, James E. *The Power of Ambition.*
  Kettering, OH: Jim Rohn International, 1993.

- Rohn, James E. *7 Strategies for Wealth and Happiness: Power Ideas from America's Foremost Business Philosopher.*
  New York: Three Rivers Press. 1996.

- Sinek, Simon. *If You Don't Understand People, You Don't Understand Business.*
  www.99u.com, 2011.

- "Spirituality." *The Oxford American College Dictionary.*
  www.oxforddictionaries.com/us/definition/american_english/, 2002.

- U.S. Census, Bureau. *Poverty Data.*
  Washington D.C. www.census.gov, 2012.

- Whyte, David. *Crossing the Unknown Sea: Work as a Pilgrimage of Identity.*
  New York: Riverhead Trade, 2002.

- "Wisdom." *The Oxford American College Dictionary.*
  www.oxforddictionaries.com/us/definition/american_english/, 2002.

www.ingramcontent.com/pod-product-compliance
Lightning Source LLC
Chambersburg PA
CBHW070108290526
45789CB00005B/1962